Praise for Ryan Thorburn's award-winning *Black 14* and *Lost Cowboys*

"I think (Black 14) is an important part of the history of Wyoming football, so it's something I visit with my staff about."
– Wyoming football coach Dave Christensen.

Casper Star-Tribune

"Lost Cowboys is particularly important to me, as I was around Laramie when the University had to shut down the baseball program in light of Title IX. Thorburn's portrayal of a long lost baseball success story is well worth the read. Now all that's left is for him to tell the world the story of the Wyoming basketball program . . .
I assume he's saving the best for last."

Amazon.com reader

Cowboy Up

Kenny Sailors, The Jump Shot and
Wyoming's Championship
Basketball History

Ryan Thorburn

Burning Daylight

Copyright © 2011 by Ryan Thorburn. All rights reserved.

Published by Burning Daylight an imprint of
Pearn and Associates, Inc.
1600 Edora Court Suite D
Fort Collins, Colorado 80525
For information about publishing please
contact happypoet@hotmail.com.

Cover design by Anne Kilgore. Photos provided as a courtesy of the University of Wyoming Sports Information Department.

Acknowledgements

Thanks to the Wyoming Sports Information Department, especially Diane Dodson and Tim Harkins, for their assistance with interviews, photos and research. Also to John R. Waggener, associate archivist at the University of Wyoming's American Heritage Center, as well as Joe Naiman, Rhett Thorburn and Phil White for their help in tracking down information and sources.

Library of Congress Control Number: 2011937193

Thorburn, Ryan 1971
Cowboy Up, by Ryan Thorburn
First edition

ISBN 978-0-9846523-0-3 paper

PRINTED IN THE UNITED STATES OF AMERICA
Canada, United Kingdom, Europe, and Australia

First edition

In memory of Ed McPherson

Contents

Foreword: Pokes Have Always Been Dazzling – *vii*

Chapter 1: Hell's Half Acre to MSG – 1

Chapter 2: Wyoming vs. the World – 11

Chapter 3: The Father of Wyoming Basketball – 20

Chapter 4: Strannigan and the Soaring '60s – 33

Chapter 5: Black Pioneers Opened the Door – 43

Chapter 6: The Jump Shot is Born – 50

Chapter 7: The Mythical Cowboy – 59

Photo section – 66

Chapter 8: Built for the Final Four – 72

Chapter 9: The "Dazzling" Dembo Days – 82

Chapter 10: The Dome of Doom – 98

Chapter 11: "I Still Get Cold Shivers" – 113

Chapter 12: Shyatt Happens . . . Again – 124

Chapter 13: Shining Star of a Storied Program – 130

Sources – 140

Marcus Bailey cuts down the net after Wyoming wins the Mountain West title in 2002.

Pokes Have Always Been Dazzling

Wyoming basketball is Fennis Dembo sitting on top of the rim at the Arena-Auditorium with his arms up in the air. It's Marcus Bailey hitting a season-saving 3-pointer with an NCAA Tournament bid on the line. It's Theo Ratliff returning a jump shot to sender. It's Jim Brandenburg seeing something in Bill Garnett and Eric Leckner no one else did. It's Adam Waddell getting off the floor with a smile on his face after a death-defying dunk gone awry. It's Jon Sommers locking down Reggie Miller with a trip to the Sweet 16 on the line. It's a Benny Dees one-liner. It's the enduring voices of Dave Walsh and Kevin McKinney coming through an old car radio. It's a Josh Davis you tube clip. It's a homemade rebound counter for Reggie Slater. It's opponents running straight into the 7,220-foot Wyoming wall in the second half.

It's certainly Kenny Sailors.

There are many reasons why I decided to write a book about the storied history of Cowboys' basketball. The most inspired being the fact that the greatest source imaginable on the subject – a man who invented the jump shot, led Wyoming to the NCAA championship in 1943 and became the program's only three-time All-American – is alive, well and happy to tell the tale. Sailors, 90 years old as I pound this keyboard, was gracious enough to sit down and share his amazing stories with me during several lengthy chats in his Laramie apartment. That's like interviewing James Madison about the Constitution, The Beatles about rock and roll, or Ernest Hemingway about writing short stories. I was fortunate enough to have a similar experience with legendary Wyoming baseball coach Bud Daniel, a World War II veteran like Sailors, for the book *Lost Cowboys*. I grew up a fan of many of the subjects in this new book, but listening to Sailors telling stories was the most rewarding experience in researching and writing *Cowboy Up*. Listening to Sailors' recollections of life on the farm in Hillsdale, Wyoming, where he instinctively left his feet to shoot a basketball as a kid so his older brother Bud would stop blocking it, to beating Georgetown and St. John's at Madison Square Garden, was an amazing opportunity. This project will be a success if in some small way it helps Kenny get into the Naismith Memorial Basketball Hall of Fame and/or the National Collegiate Basketball Hall of Fame, hopefully while he's still with us.

Another motivation was to remind or educate people, including some Mountain West and younger Wyoming fans, that the Cowboys have an amazing hoops tradition that includes a Hall of Fame head coach (Ev Shelton), two national championships (if you weren't aware of that fact, you're in for a nice surprise in the second chapter), 15 different All-Americans, and 22 conference championships. I've covered basketball games everywhere from New York's Madison Square Garden to the Staples Center in downtown Los Angeles. I've experienced old Ivy League gyms (Harvard's Lavietes Pavilion) and shiny new arenas in Big 12 country (Mizzou Arena in Columbia, the Sprint Center in Kansas City). I've been to Allen Fieldhouse in Lawrence, Gallagher-Iba in Stillwater, The Pit in Albuquerque and the Lahaina Civic Center at the Maui Invitational. You won't find a more electric atmosphere or a greater home-court advantage than inside the Arena-Auditorium (at least when the state is excited about the Cowboys). Long before the "Dome of Doom," there was Hell's Half Acre Gym, where Wyoming compiled a 222-44 record from 1924-51. The overflow crowds and national success led to construction of the equally intimidating War Memorial Fieldhouse. Jim Brandenburg's 1980-81 WAC championship team went undefeated in the old barn, including an 86-84 double-overtime victory over Brigham Young University. After the game, the scornful visiting coach, Frank Arnold, described the Wyoming faithful as "despicable."

Despicably good fans who love their Cowboys.

Wyoming also has great tradition in football, which is documented in my first book, *Black 14*. The Cowboys were BCS busters long before Boise State fielded a Division I program with appearances in the Sugar and Fiesta Bowls. There isn't a better place to be on a fall Saturday afternoon than War Memorial Stadium. Basketball, however, has been Wyoming's best sport through the decades. Even during the program's recent struggles, fans in the Equality State have still had something to cheer about thanks to the Cowgirls. As a kid, I remember the smell of the tanbark at the Fieldhouse and watching mythical figures like Charles Bradley and Mike Jackson playing above the rim. Growing up in Casper, Wyoming, I remember the Events Center being sold out as Dembo-mania spread throughout the state and eventually reached the national spotlight. As an undergraduate at Wyoming, I sat in the front row of the students' section watching Tim Breaux,

Slater, Ratliff and other resplendent players tease us with their individual talents while the team fell short of realizing their NCAA Tournament dreams. I watched in horror as Queint Higgins and Bailey each suffered program-altering knee injuries during blowout wins. As a reporter for the *Casper Star-Tribune*, I had a chance to cover most of Larry Shyatt's games during his successful but short-lived first stint with the Cowboys. More recently at the *Boulder Camera*, I got to know Steve McClain, an under-appreciated coach and a good man, who gave Wyoming its last taste of March Madness a decade ago before joining the University of Colorado staff. But getting a chance to revisit the past with Pokes pioneers like Keith Bloom, Tony Windis, Curt Jimerson, Brandenburg and Sailors was the real thrill.

Wyoming basketball has always been dazzling.

– Ryan Thorburn

Charles Bradley dunks the ball over an opponent at War Memorial Fieldhouse.

Hell's Half Acre to MSG

New York City's Madison Square Garden, dubbed by the press as "The World's Most Famous Arena," is often referred to by today's coaches and players as the Mecca of basketball. Oscar Robinson. Bill Bradley. Willis Reed. Chris Mullin. Patrick Ewing. Reggie Miller. Michael Jordan. LeBron James. Many of the greatest players in the game's history have saved their best performances for the New York stage. No player had the crowds buzzing and jaws dropping at the old Madison Square Garden quite like Kenny Sailors in the early 1940s. Wyoming's only three-time All-American dazzled the East Coast fans and media by introducing them to the jump shot while leading the 1942-43 Cowboys to an NCAA championship and then a victory over National Invitation Tournament champion St. John's. Decades before Fennis Dembo graced the cover of *Sports Illustrated* as "A Dazzling Dude," the scribes at *Time*, *Life* and the New York papers were chronicling the amazing story of Sailors and the Wyoming basketball program.

Almost 70 years after earning the Chuck Taylor Award as college basketball's best player and being named most Most Outstanding Player of the NCAA Tournament, Sailors can still recall those glory days when the 'Pokes were the big story in the Big Apple as if they happened last March. Now 90, Sailors resides in a small apartment in Laramie, Wyoming, just steps away from War Memorial Stadium on the University of Wyoming campus. The living legend attends all of the home games, Cowboys and Cowgirls, at the Arena-Auditorium where his number 4 jersey and the NCAA championship banner hang from the rafters. Wyoming basketball has a rich tradition – producing great players, coaches and teams sporadically throughout the decades – but nothing has ever matched the March Madness the homegrown Cowboys created at Madison Square Garden in 1943.

"You can imagine the first time when I went in there. They announce your name when you go on the court: 'Kenny Sailors from Wyoming,'" Sailors said. "And the crowd, they're going nuts. I've never seen anything like it in my life. That's more people than I ever saw in a building in my life. Never even come close to it probably."

Some of the best basketball in Wyoming history took place during Ev Shelton's practices when Sailors first stepped on campus (freshmen were not allowed to play on the varsity at that time). The Cowboys had some pretty noteworthy upperclassmen –

including Curt Gowdy, Bud Kerback, Willie Rothman and Bill Strannigan – but it was hard to ignore the spunk and talent oozing from Sailors and classmates Jim Collins, Lou Roney, Floyd Volker and Jimmy Weir.

"We got kind of cocky because Shelton scrimmaged us with the varsity. We played against them as freshmen, and I could get by any of them. And they knew it. So could Weir," Sailors says with an ornery look in his eye.

"We got to teasing the varsity and saying, 'We could beat you guys any day of the week.' And we believed we could. They'd razz us and say, 'You couldn't beat us in a million years,' and on and on. Shelton was hearing all of this and he got tired of it. He says, 'You crazy freshmen think you can beat my varsity? I'll just arrange a game and let the public come in and watch it.' He didn't think we could.

"We played the game and beat 'em. We didn't just beat 'em, we beat 'em by 12 or 15 points at Hells Half Acre. And Shelton said, 'Well, maybe I've got something.' Because he did. That's where it started."

A year later, when the 1940-41 season tipped off with Wyoming pummeling Northern Colorado (then called Colorado State Teachers College) 57-55 in the opener in Laramie, Shelton decided to ease Sailors and the group of super sophomores into the rotation. The Cowboys finished the regular season with a 14-4 record and captured the first of the program's eight Skyline Conference (also known as the Mountain States Conference and Big Seven) championships during Shelton's Hall of Fame career. The well-traveled Cowboys won road games at Oklahoma City, Texas Tech, Northern Colorado, Colorado State, Utah, Utah State and Colorado.

"Shelton knew Weir and I were a little cocky and he did probably the best thing in never starting us as sophomores," Sailors admits. "We had both been all-state (in high school) in football and basketball. Shelton figured we were a little too cocky."

In the first round of the NCAA Tournament at Municipal Auditorium in Kansas City, Missouri, Wyoming lost 52-40 to Arkansas on March 21, 1941. The next day in the consolation round, Wyoming dropped a 45-44 heart-breaker to Creighton. Sailors watched helplessly from the bench for the most part. Gowdy, Rothman and Strannigan were the stars of the team. Ironically, Arkansas' star player, "Jumpin'" Johnny Adams, was also one of the pioneers of the jump shot. The 6-3 All-American led the Razorbacks to a win over the Cowboys and a trip to the Final Four with Sailors riding the pine until the outcome was all but decided.

At that time, the fledgling NCAA Tournament invited only eight teams and did its best to make sure the preeminent teams from each region were included. Dartmouth, North Carolina, Pittsburgh and Wisconsin made up the East Region with Arkansas, Creighton, Washington State and Wyoming included from the West Region. The Razorbacks had gone unbeaten in the Southwest Conference that season, the first team to accomplish that feat, with their "Eiffel Tower" lineup, which included 6-foot-8 center John "Treetop" Freiberger, 6-7 forward Gordon "Shorty" Carpenter, and 6-4 guard R.C. Pitts. But Adams was the star scoring machine with his unguardable leaping shot.

"Johnny Adams was a great All-American. Weir and I didn't start and we didn't get too much playing time. We just hung tight and knew this whole bunch was graduating the next year," Sailors said. "But we were getting beat pretty bad by Arkansas, and Shelton put Weir and I in, and we went wild. We could have beaten Arkansas under certain circumstances. I got a lot of publicity out of that game."

Wyoming Governor Nels Smith was rumored to have hastily excused himself from an important meeting in Denver so he could get up to Fort Collins, Colorado, in time for the Poke's 40-34 victory over the Aggies of Colorado A & M on Feb. 7, 1941. He sat on Shelton's bench as an honorary team captain on March 21, 1941, while Sailors dazzled the crowd with his dribbling and shooting skills in the second half of the program's first NCAA Tournament game.

The University of Wyoming's yearbook includes the following recap of Shelton's second season in Laramie:

Coach Ev Shelton, in his second year as head basketball coach at Wyoming University, expertly guided his Punchers to the top rung in the Big Seven ladder of supremacy. And the man at the helm is only beginning. The championship team was a group of hustling sophomores and juniors with only two seniors on the squad and only one in the starting lineup.

The club was the most popular in the history of Wyoming sports annals. All attendance records fell by the wayside as every town and ranch in Wyoming begged for tickets. At every home game many disappointed fans were turned away. There is no question what made this team so popular. It was not merely the fact that it won games; not merely because Coach Shelton had turned out the smoothest piece of basketball machinery most fans ever saw.

No the reason was pride; pride of Wyoming products. Yes, the home town boys made good. Every man of the squad of 11 was a Wyoming product. Each had been famous in his own right on a Wyoming high school five.

So thus it is rightly "Wyoming against the world." Shelton and his eleven Wyomingites played against men from every other part of the country and not once were they overshadowed, not even in defeat.

Strannigan, a talented player from Rock Springs, Wyoming, was named as a Chuck Taylor first-team All-American in 1941 after leading the Cowboys in scoring (200 points, 10.5 per game). Shelton wisely decided to let Sailors move into spotlight in the seasons to come. It was far from a one-man show. The Cowboys' roster was loaded with great players, including Milo Komenich, one of the only out-of-state recruits Shelton went after. The center from Gary, Indiana, paced Wyoming in scoring during the 1941-42 campaign (222 points, 11.7 per game).

"Komenich was the best big man, in my opinion, in the nation," Sailors said. "There were others who got a lot of publicity on the East Coast, but they couldn't handle old Milo."

After back-to-back wins at Montana and Montana State to open the season, the Cowboys made the long journey to the East Coast in late December of 1941 and early January of 1942 to play road games against Canisius (lost 56-44), CCNY (won 49-43), Baltimore (won 52-35), Albright (won 73-54) and Duquesne (lost 46-30). Wyoming beat Utah at Hell's Half Acre upon returning from the grueling seven-game road trip. The brief appearance in Laramie was followed by three consecutive conference road defeats at Brigham Young, Utah and Colorado before the Pokes rattled off nine consecutive wins to end the season. A 15-5 record wasn't enough, however, to earn a trip to the 1942 NCAA Tournament. But Shelton's philosophy of playing anybody, anywhere, anytime would pay dividends.

"I just get so disgusted with these young coaches today talking about how tough it is to play on the road. I put it this way: If you can beat a team on your home court, you can beat them anywhere," Sailors said. "There's no difference in these courts – the free throw line is the same distance from the baseline, the courts are the same length, the same width, the referees are the same, the balls are the same, the rules are the same. The only difference is if you can't stand to play before a crowd when your mom and dad aren't there and your friends aren't there. And they boo you. If that's your problem then you shouldn't be playing college ball, because they're going to boo you every place you go.

"Shelton used to tell us, 'Don't get uptight about the booing. They never boo a bum. If they think you can beat them, then they're going to be booing you. And if they're ahead of us by 20 points, they won't be booing you, they'll be putting their coats on to go home and beat the traffic.' I found that to be true."

The 1942-43 Cowboys were truly a Wyoming team. Sailors and Collins had graduated from Laramie High School. Volker and Earl "Shadow" Ray were from Casper, Wyoming, Roney from Powell, Wyoming, and Weir from Green River, Wyoming, Jimmie Reese and Antone Katana were from Rock Springs, Wyoming James Darden and Kenneth Tallman were from Cheyenne, Wyoming Vernon Jensen was from Lyman, Wyoming. In addition to Komenich, the Hoosiers State export, the other players on the roster not from the state were Don Waite (Scottsbluff, Nebraska), Charlie Castle (Phoenix, Arizona), and Jack Downey (Phoenix, Arizona).

Before this band of brothers went their separate ways to fight in World War II, these Cowboys forever made Wyoming an important part of college basketball history with one of the great runs ever witnessed at Madison Square Garden.

"Shelton even got to thinking before that season that we were a special group," Sailors said. "In '43 he began to think, 'These kids must have a little something on the ball.'"

Wyoming opened the remarkable journey with three consecutive wins over an all-star team from Fort Warren (two of the games were played on the road, the other in Laramie). Another grueling road trip – nine games this time – began with a loss at Duquesne on Dec. 23, 1942. The Cowboys responded with a 23-game winning streak that began with a 56-52 victory at Albright on Dec. 24, 1942, and was not snapped until a 41-33 loss to the Denver Legion team on March 19, 1943. By then, Shelton's boys had already won the Skyline Conference and were fine-tuning the machine for the program's second appearance in the NCAA Tournament.

"We beat Phillips 66, who were the national champs, twice on their own court," Sailors said of the classic 42-41 (overtime) and 37-36 Wyoming victories on Feb. 2-3, 1943, over the AAU powerhouse, which was essentially a professional team comprised of former All-Americans. "They wouldn't come here, so Shelton says, 'OK, we'll play you twice on your home court.' So we played 'em in Enid, Oklahoma. Shelton wanted us to play these teams because he felt you had to play teams better than you are if you're ever going to be a great ball club. We played and beat the national AAU champions, and after that we kind of felt we were a good team. We thought if we could beat them, we could beat anyone.

"Of course, Shelton had pounded that thinking into us from our freshman year. He said, 'You can beat anyone if you make up your mind to do it.'"

Wyoming beat the University of Denver 58-45 the day after the defeat of the Denver Legion team to finish the regular season with a 27-2 record. The Cowboys opened up the NCAA Tournament with a 53-50 victory over Oklahoma on March 26, 1943, back in Kansas City. Komenich led the way with 22 points, and Weir added 14 against the Sooners. The next day, Wyoming edged Texas, 58-54 in the national semifinals, to earn a trip to the title game in New York. Komenich (17 points) and Weir (13 points) highlighted the stat sheet again. Many of the Pokes would say later that this was the best team they played en route to the national title. Longhorns All-American John "Shotgun" Hargis – who also led Texas to a Final Four appearance in 1947 after serving in the war and won a National Basketball League championship with the Anderson Packers (1948-49) – scored a game-high 29 points against the Cowboys.

"They were good teams," Sailors said. "We didn't beat 'em by much, but we beat 'em."

Half Acre Gym was a heavenly basketball gem at the time of its dedication on Jan. 23, 1925. Wyoming beat Utah that night, 31-29 in overtime, to christen the new gym. The facility – which became known as Hell's Half Acre due to the torment most visiting teams suffered through on the scoreboard – cost $150,000 to build and was the largest, most modern basketball home between Syracuse and California.

"Hell's Half Acre had one of the biggest playing courts in America at that time, and we used to run teams to death there," Gowdy is quoted as saying in the Wyoming basketball media guide. "Teams died at the altitude, and we could play with anyone. Even the name, Hell's Half Acre, made it memorable."

The capacity of Half Acre Gym was just over 4,000, and the Cowboys routinely exceeded that number during the Sailors era.

"These fans, you can't believe it. They were crazy," Sailors recalled of the atmosphere during his playing days. "They packed 5,000 or 6,000 in Half Acre when it probably should have only held 3,500. They'd bring trains in from Evanston and Green River and Rock Springs and Rawlins. They'd even stop at Rock River, or any place people wanted to get on. Then they brought buses down from Sheridan and way up north and east. We always filled the gym, and the overflow crowd would listen to the game in the theater or the student union. Then after the game, the players would have to go over there and shake hands with the people. It was quite a deal for a bunch of country kids."

During Sailors' four seasons in uniform, Wyoming posted a 31-2 record at Half Acre Gym. Both losses were during the 1945-46 campaign when the All-American returned from World War II to exhaust his eligibility and complete his education. In the spring of 1943, the Cowboys finished 9-0 in Laramie, culminating with three consecutive victories over Brigham Young University from Feb. 25-27, by scores of 53-42, 47-43 and 66-43. Wyoming played road games at Howard-Payne, the Colorado School of Mines, Poudre Valley, Denver Legion and Denver before heading to Kansas City for the NCAA Tournament. After dispatching the Sooners and Longhorns, Sailors and the boys took the show back to New York to face Georgetown for the NCAA title.

"I can't explain it to you," Sailors said of what the experience was like. "They told us to dress like cowboys, so we did – big hats, bright shirts, handkerchief, cowboy boots. We walked down Times Square four or five abreast, and people would walk around us and be looking at us. We got a big charge out of that because we were a cocky bunch of kids."

The confident Cowboys backed up the swagger with a 46-34 victory over the Hoyas. Sailors led Wyoming with 19 points, using the jump shot at times while also showing off his Bob Cousy-like dribbling skills. Komenich added nine points. No players on Georgetown scored more than six points.

"I have been coaching basketball for 20 years. I have handled other teams that apparently were the equal of my current squad physically, but never have I had a band of boys whose team spirit was such that you could almost see it and feel it," Shelton said in the April 3, 1943, edition of the *Laramie Daily Bulletin*. "In every game, I felt that that spirit gave us a sixth man on the floor."

Joe Cummisky, the sports editor of the *New York PM* newspaper, described the championship game this way:

> As far as the NCAA basketball tournament is concerned, the Sailors has landed and has the situation well in hand. Before you get too confused, let me hasten to explain that Wyoming University's Cowboy cagers are the National Collegiate AA champions, and they owe it mostly to the dribble and all-around court savvy of a blond kid named Kenny Sailors, who picked the Cowboys up by their high-heeled boots in the Garden Tuesday to out game and – more important – outscore Georgetown in the East-West finals, 46-34.
>
> You'll get another chance to see this NCAA championship in action Thursday night – if you hurry. It is playing St. John's University of Brooklyn in the same Garden, for the benefit of the Red Cross. The winner of that one should qualify for the World Series, the backstroke in Hawaii, and Mayor La Guardia's discarded 10-gallon hats, because if that game doesn't decide once and for all the mythical championship of these United States, make mine bingo.
>
> The crowd of 13,206 Tuesday saw some tingling basketball for 30 minutes. But at the time there were 10 minutes left, Wyoming decided to show everyone why it came east. The score then was 31-31. Big Milo Komenich, Wyoming center, caged a deuce, and then Collins hit again. Milo came right back to add two more, and Sailors added a foul shot to make it 38 for Wyoming. Georgetown, meanwhile, had gathered three points and missed four more, but that didn't interfere with the Wyoming plans at all. Milo hit again and again, and Sailors added another, and pretty soon it was all over – 46-34 – before Georgetown could take a deep breath and holler Hoya!
>
> I started out to land on Sailors with my adjectives and I'd like to explain before the final whistle. This Sailors can do everything with a basketball but tie a seaman's knot, and given time and a chance to dribble two steps, he'd probably be able to do that.
>
> Sailors was the hand who held the S. S. Wyoming together when everybody was figuring Georgetown was in. I think someone was holding Director Ned Irish from rushing onto the court to present the NCAA mug, but it was explained later he was just trying to make a fast getaway to the box office to catch the early departures and sell them tickets for the Red Cross game.
>
> It's enough to say that Sailors – also voted the most valuable player in the NCAA final as a sort of anti-climactic gesture – is quite a ball player, and if Georgetown had one who faintly resembled him the game might have been a few points closer.

Two nights later, on April 1, 1943, Wyoming proved the NCAA title was no joke, beating hometown St. John's, the 1943 National Invitation Tournament winners, 52-47 in overtime. The Red Cross charity game also served to prove which tournament winner was the true national champion.

"That was an interesting game," Sailors said. "St. John's caught up with us and tied the game with five seconds left (in regulation). When they made that last basket, we knew you could fast break if you grabbed that ball after the basket, so we threw that long pass down the court. The referee, old Kennedy was his name, blew his whistle until his cheeks puffed out and said that (St. John's coach) Joe Lapchick had already called timeout the moment they made the basket. Shelton said, 'They don't have the right to call a timeout because we can grab that ball and hit a fast break if they're not back.' I got the basket. I dribbled down in four or five seconds and made the basket before the game was over. The crowd went crazy, but they called it back. And the crowd booed, so a lot of them didn't agree with Kennedy. And Shelton says, 'Well, there's nothing we can do.'"

So the witnesses at Madison Square Garden were treated to an overtime session. It would prove to be Wyoming's time.

"Komenich had fouled out, and Weir was tickled to death. It was the first time he really got to be the center. He had been all-state three years in Wyoming and had been the best (center) we'd had up until that time," Sailors said. "All I said to him was, 'OK, big boy, get in there and I'll throw you the ball.' The first three passes I threw to him he scored. He was fast, probably the fastest big man in the nation. Weir came out to the high post and (Harry) Boykoff was dumb enough, as slow as he was at 7-foot, to come out and try to cover Weir. It was pitiful. The game was over. Weir made two layups and they fouled him the third time."

Sailors, who had scored 28 points against BYU and 27 against Utah earlier in the season, led the Pokes with 16 points against Georgetown. Komenich had 20 points before fouling out against St. John's, while Weir finished off the win with 13 points. For the season, Komenich (16.5 ppg), Sailors (15.0 ppg) and Weir (10.0 ppg) all averaged double figures in scoring. Wyoming averaged 59.4 points per game as a team while holding the opposition to 39.5 points per game.

The Wyoming yearbook captured the unequaled celebration in the Equality State that spring with these words:

> After Wyoming's win of the national collegiate championship, the state's ten-gallon hat sailed sky-high, and the Cowboy team was welcomed back to Laramie and the University with an all-out reception.
>
> Impromptu celebrations broke out all over the campus and city, and a Victory holiday was declared for University students, while Laramie merchants closed their stores for a half-day in their honor.
>
> The team's return was celebrated with a parade and banquet, with many notables of the state in attendance.
>
> Climax of the festivities came with an all-University assembly, at which each member of the team was introduced and Governor Leslie C. Hunt gave the keynote address.

The Wyoming Cowboys were the national kings of college basketball, as documented in the April 12, 1943, edition of "Time Magazine":

> Like St. John's, whose basketball more than supports all other sports, Wyoming is a basketball college and this was its biggest year. To match the Indians' (Harry 'Big Boy') Boykoff, the Cowboys had 6 ft 7 Milo Komenich, like Boykoff one of the season's leading scorers (401 points) and one of the few Eiffel-tower basketballers who can really play the game. The Cowboys also had a supporting cast all at least 6 ft. 3 – with one exception. The exception, a little dynamo named Kenny Sailors, made it tough for St. John's.
>
> While Giants Boykoff (17 points) and Komenich (20 points) battled each other almost to a standoff, Sailors was all over the court, again & again drove like a P-38 through the St. John's team to pour the ball through the basket....
>
> In the five-minute overtime period Wyoming anticlimactically picked up the ball and threw in five points to win, 52-to-47. By that time the crowd was beyond all feeling.

A dark cloud hung over the hoopla surrounding Wyoming's national title. The team would not get a chance to repeat as the University suspended the program in 1943-44 due to World War II. In the days and weeks after returning to Laramie from New York as conquering hardwood heroes, most of the Cowboys, including Sailors, would be trading in their Chuck Taylors and basketball jerseys for military uniforms to enter the fray of combat. Some of them wouldn't be coming home.

Wyoming vs. the World

Wyoming can feel like one big hometown. If a person from the state spots someone wearing a Cowboys hat or shirt with the distinctive "Steamboat" logo – whether they're traveling abroad in Paris or London, sightseeing in New York or San Francisco, or just grinding through life in Denver (as so many University of Wyoming graduates do) – the image serves as an invitation to strike up a conversation. And, more times than not, no matter what town in Wyoming the parties are from, they usually have mutual friends, or at least friends of friends, and are able to share similar stories. One of the main reasons for the connection, besides the fact that Wyoming is the least-populated state in the Union, is a love of the University of Wyoming, the state's only four-year institution of higher learning, and the Cowboys.

There are loyal fans known to drive 385 miles east from Jackson, or nearly five hours south from Sheridan on slick highways to see the Pokes play on the High Plains of Laramie. And after the final buzzer sounds, they typically drive straight home in the wee hours. Ask any of these devoted supporters who the best coach in the proud history of the basketball program is and, depending on their age, the answer will either be Ev Shelton or Jim Brandenburg. Best player in school history? Kenny Sailors or Flynn Robinson or Charles Bradley or Fennis Dembo or Marcus Bailey . . . again, the answer will depend on what year the person's fandom was born.

But even the most die-hard Cowboys followers tend to be stumped by the following:

Q. Which Wyoming head coach has the greatest winning percentage?

A. Willard "Dutch" Witte.

Q. When did Wyoming win its first national championship?

A. During the 1933-34 season.

Shelton, a member of the Naismith Memorial Basketball Hall of Fame, is known as "The Father of Cowboy Basketball." That makes Witte the program's grandfather. Witte compiled an astonishing 134-51 (.724) record from 1931-39, winning five Rocky Mountain Athletic Conference East Division titles and two conference championships in nine seasons on the bench. During the 1933-34 season, the Cowboys posted 20 consecutive wins and finished with a 26-3 record. Wyoming was later named the 1934 national champions by the Helms Athletic Foundation, the only collegiate voting poll of the era. Witte produced Wyoming's first All-Americans, as his starting five on the 1934 squad – Ed McGinty, Art Haman, John Kimball, Haskell Leuty and Les Witte – were so honored by the AAU.

Under "Dutch" Witte, described as a reserved, shy gentleman, the Cowboys won 52 consecutive games against RMAC East Division opponents in the Half Acre Gym. He also coached Wyoming football for six seasons, although not as successfully, finishing with a 16-30-3 record on the gridiron from 1933-38. Witte later served as director of the Wyoming athletics program and was a member of the National Basketball Association Rules Committee. Despite all of these notable accomplishments, the 1934 team does not have a Helms Foundation national title banner hanging in the Arena-Auditorium next to the 1943 NCAA championship banner.

"We haven't done much to honor that group," said longtime Wyoming Sports Information Director and current Associate Athletic Director Kevin McKinney. "You say, 'Well, they had a great year and they were picked (as national champions), but they didn't do it on the floor against somebody in a championship.' That's true, but they didn't have a (NCAA) championship then. It wasn't their fault. They might have got on the floor and got beaten, or they might have got on the floor and won it like the '43 team . . . .

"I think there should be a banner. We want to try and do that for those guys."

There is, however, a banner hanging in honor of Wyoming's 2007 Women's National Invitation Tournament championship team. Since 2003, while the men's program has struggled to compete in the Mountain West, Joe Legerski's Cowgirls have been a bright spot during some dark times at the Arena-Auditorium in Laramie.

Wyoming earned its "Equality State" nickname after becoming the first territory to pass the Suffrage Act into law on Dec. 10, 1869, extending the right to vote for women. Fittingly, the first basketball team to compete at the University was also female.

According to a 1951 article written by the late Dr. Robert H. Burns – the former head of Wyoming's Wool Department and the leading scorer on the 1918-19 and 1919-20 Cowboys teams coached by John Corbett – an effort was made to start a girls team in 1903 with several closed-door "practice games" held. In January of 1903, the Wyoming State Legislature appropriated $15,000 to construct a gymnasium with a capacity of 1,000. Soon after its completion, "The Gym," became known as Little Red Gym, due to the color of the exterior bricks.

On Jan. 20, 1905, two girl's teams, the Reds and the Yellows, put on an exhibition in the new facility. Final score: Reds 9, Yellows 8. On Feb. 13, the Yellows beat the Reds, 11-10. Laura Breisch was the star of the Reds. Her teammates included Miriam Corthell, Mildred McIntosh, Anna Reid, Edith Betts and Neva Nelson. Ida Langheldt led the Yellows, along with Ethel Punting, Marg McIntosh, Grace Peabody, Gertie Punting and Abbie Drew.

During the Alumni Banquet that spring, Brown-Eyed Susans were in bloom on campus and it was suggested that the University adopt the beautiful look of the brown and yellow flowers as the school colors. And so the original, unofficial, Cowgirls uniforms included a yellow 'W' over a brown background worn over their middies, along with long black bloomers. On Feb. 17, 1905, Wyoming beat the Farmer Girls in a scorcher played in Fort Collins, 7-6.

A little over 103 years later, Legerski's Cowgirls made their first appearance in the women's NCAA Tournament.

The first documented men's game in the Little Red Gym, a facility described at the time as the "pride and joy of the whole school," was an exhibition between the varsity and junior varsity on March 24, 1905. The first official game in the program's history was a 17-5 victory over the Laramie Town Team on April 21, 1905. The Cowboys' starting five was listed as: forwards Downey and D. Hunton, center Nelson, guards G. Muir and Sellon.

W. Yates, the Cowboys' original head coach, compiled a 4-2 record from 1905-06. Lt. Coburn (5-7, 1907-08), Elmer G. Hoefer (3-3, 1909), Harold I. Dean (9-13, 1909-12), Leon C. Excelby (2-5, 1913) and Ralph Thacker (3-7, 1914-15) all guided Wyoming for brief stints during the fledgling years before Corbett brought some stability with a 37-41 record over his nine seasons (1916-24).

Dr. Burns, an avid historian of the Rocky Mountain West, began keeping athletic statistics for Wyoming. The individual records in the modern Wyoming basketball media guides date back to 1910, when Oscar Prestegard led the Pokes in scoring at 15.2 points per game (76 points in five games played). Fulton Bellamy only played in three games from 1915-16 but averaged 20.5 points over that span. The next player to average over 20 points for a season was the legendary Joe Capua, who scored 637 points in 26 games (24.5 per) during the 1955-56 season. Bellamy's wife, Willamena, established a scholarship to honor her husband, who received a degree in civil engineering from Wyoming. Prior to World War II, he worked with Bellamy and Sons in Laramie and was an assistant state engineer. During the War, he was an instructor in the Department of Civil Engineering. Following the War, he became an airport engineer with the FAA in Kansas City. He went on to become the Midwest District Airport Engineer in charge of all airport construction in the area, including the construction of O'Hare Airport in Chicago.

Milward Simpson, the only athlete in Wyoming history to captain the football, baseball and basketball teams, led the Cowboys in scoring with an average of 11.6 points per game in 1917-18. The future U.S. Senator and Wyoming Governor played with Burns, Lloyd Buchanan, Robert Fitske, Ray Lundgren, Fred Layman, Oscar Larson and Ralph McWhinnie. The highlight of the group's run on the hardwood together, and the Corbett era of basketball, was a 10-1 finish to the 1919-20 campaign, which included an 8-0 record at Little Red Gym and road triumphs over Colorado State (30-10) and Northern Colorado (38-27). The only blemish was a 28-19 loss at the Colorado School of Mines. The season was recapped as follows in the Wyoming yearbook:

Only one game has been lost during the season, and when the Cowboys went down to Colorado for a little visit they upset all the Colorado dope with their fast passing and wonderful defense . . . .

Burns will have completed four years of stellar basketball this year, and it's with deepest regret that the school sees him leave the floor.

According to historical documentation found at the University of Wyoming's American Heritage Center, located across the street from the Arena-Auditorium, Burns was born August 23, 1900, on the Flag Ranch nine miles south of Laramie. After graduating from Wyoming in 1920, Burns obtained his M.A. from Iowa State and his Ph. D. in Edinburgh, Scotland. He taught at Wyoming and later worked with the U.S. Department of Agriculture and served as consultant to the Iranian government in New York. He wrote for numerous publications over the years, including articles for the *Laramie Republican-Boomerang* about the ranch industry. Burns died in an automobile accident on June 14, 1973.

Corbett, once called Wyoming's "Grand Old Man of Athletics," had a lot to do with producing student-athletes who went on to accomplish great achievements in their respective fields after graduating. He arrived in Laramie after earning All-American honors as a football player at Harvard (1890-93). He is considered to be the founding father of Wyoming athletics, having established the University's physical education curriculum and served as head coach of the football program (15-44-3, 1915-23). Corbett also coached Wyoming's early baseball and track teams. As the Director of Physical Education, Corbett is credited with modernizing the school's athletic facilities with the construction of Half Acre Gym, and the football playing field was called Corbett Field until War Memorial Stadium was constructed around it. He also established the state high school basketball tournament that was hosted by the University. Wyoming's physical education complex and intercollegiate swimming pool were named in his honor.

After winning just nine games over his final four seasons on the bench, Corbett stepped aside and allowed head coaches Stewart Clark (43-24, 1925-28) and George McLaren (28-10, 1929-30) to begin a winning tradition that set the table for Wyoming's first national championship.

In Willard Witte's first season as coach, the Cowboys finished the regular season with a sparkling 18-2 record, including a 13-game winning streak down the home stretch, to win the East Division of the RMAC. After beating Utah 32-25 to open a three-game playoff in Salt Lake City, the West Division champion Utes won the next two games, including a 40-39 triumph in the rubber match, to claim the conference title. The star of the team was forward Les Witte, the younger brother of Willard, who became the program's first All-American that season as recognized by Converse Yearbook and later the Helms

Foundation. Other starters of the team, dubbed the "First Five," were forward Joe Schwartz, center Jack McNiff, and guards John Kimball and Casey Rugg. In the second year of the Witte era, the group led Wyoming to an 18-2 finish. The upstart Pokes claimed the conference championship by beating Brigham Young twice in a three-game playoff hosted at Half Acre Gym on March 4-6, 1932. Wyoming started the next season 10-0, including a 42-24 romp over Stanford in Laramie, before losing to Colorado at Boulder on Feb. 2, 1933. The team captured the East Division again but lost two of three to BYU in the playoff in Provo, including a 41-39 defeat in the decisive game on March, 11, 1933. The Wyoming yearbook detailed the phenomenal first three years of Willard Witte's run as follows:

The Witte system of play has incorporated a "bullet-pass" offense, which has been the puzzle of Wichita Henry's, three times National Champions; Piggly Wiggly, conquerors of the champions; Creighton University, Missouri Valley Champions; Stanford University, one of the coast's best teams, and Rocky Mountain Conference teams for the last three years.
Besides coaching "Wyoming's most popular sport," "Dutch" has been assistant football coach, and has aided greatly in the development of the backfield men during the past three years.
Coach Witte, a graduate of Nebraska University, has acquired a record that hasn't been equaled in the annals of Conference coaching.

The Wyoming basketball program would reach even greater heights during the magical 1933-34 season. The Cowboys cruised through the RMAC, finishing 14-0 in the East Division and then sweeping the three-game playoff with West Division champions and regional rival BYU on consecutive nights from March 10-12 in Laramie.

Hail, The Champs!
Wyoming's Cowboys, Eastern division champs, won their second conference title when they defeated the Western division's best, the Brigham Young Cougars, in the three-game playoff at Laramie. The series was one of the most exciting in years, and the Punchers had to play real basketball to grab the crown.
Wyoming won the first game, 43-38. The tilt was even all the way and Wyoming had just enough margin to take the first victory.
The second game was the real thriller. With ten minutes to play Wyoming was 12 points behind, but the Punchers put on the pressure, and in one of the greatest rallies ever seen on the big floor, brought the count up

to a 42-42 tie when the final gun sounded. In the extra period, Wyoming scored five markers to the Cougars' two, and won the champion- ship, 47-44.

Both teams took things easier in the third game, with nothing at stake. Wyoming controlled the game all the way, winning 44-35, even without Les Witte, who was injured.

The next night, Wyoming began play at the national AAU tournament in Kansas City. The Pokes beat Belen, New Mexico (58-11), the Wilcox Oilers (43-20), the Gridley Oilers (28-25), Reno Creamery (39-35) and Utah State (39-35) before losing to the Tulsa Diamond X Oilers (29-29) in what was the ninth game in as many nights for Wyoming.

The best college basketball team in America! That is the title earned by the Cowboys as they placed second in the national AAU tournament at Kansas City where they were named the most popular team on the floor.

The Punchers started out by trouncing the Belen, New Mexico, quintet by a score of 58-11. Then they took the Wilcox Oilers of Topeka by a 43-20 count. Meeting the Ogden Boosters in their next game, Wyoming's basketeers trailed 31-11 at the end of the half, but staged one of the greatest comebacks in the history of the game to win, 39-35.

Another second half rally won a game for the Punchers, when they defeated the Gridley Motors of Wichita, 28-25, in a fast final quarter. In the semi-finals they defeated the Hutchinson Renos, 30-27.

Wyoming's glorious bid for a national championship fell short, when the Cowboys lost to the Tulsa Oilers in the final game, by a count of 29-19. The Punchers started out with the lead, but tiring from playing nine games in ten days, they went down to defeat.

The Cowboys concluded the season with two anti-climactic charity exhibition games against Piggly Wiggly that were played in Casper. Wyoming lost 35-29 and 31-29 to the AAU Pigs. And then the postseason honors began to roll in.

Les Witte, whose weapon of choice was a left-handed hook shot, became the first two-time All-American in Wyoming history and was the first player in the program to score over 1,000 points for a career (1,069). He remains the only player to lead the program in scoring four straight seasons. Witte was a star athlete at Lincoln Nebraska High School where the football team went 23-0-2 during his playing days (1927-30) and the basketball team racked up a 40-10 record en route to the Nebraska state championship. The *Spalding Guide,* an early sports magazine published from 1889 to 1939, once wrote about the original Wyoming basketball star in a 1932 issue:

"Witte was the cleverest player to show in the conference in a long time. This boy's dribbling, pivoting and feinting, and his left hand arch shots, could not be stopped."

The team's other starters in 1933-34 – Ed McGinty, Art Haman, John Kimball and Haskell Leuty – were also named as AAU All-Americans. McGinty, after three years as a sub, was the unit's ball-hawking defensive forward and a "long-shot artist." Haman, a guard, was a clever ball-handler and passer. Kimball was a versatile guard and a four-time all-conference selection. Leuty, a tall Texan, was the Cowboys' all-conference center. Willard "Buzz" West, Jack Bugas, Stan Christensen, Lloyd Dowler and Ken Rugg were the other members of the squad.

"I was a rabid Cowboy basketball fan as a boy growing up in Cheyenne," Curt Gowdy, who played at Wyoming for Ev Shelton from 1940-42 before becoming one of American's most recognizable broadcasting voices, said after being inducted into his alma mater's athletics hall of fame. "I used to watch games in Half Acre from the balcony with my legs hanging over the edge. Les Witte and Ed McGinty were some of my favorite players to watch."

When the team returned to campus after nearly winning the national AAU tournament, the Cowboys were "looking wan and drawn from their week of exhausting play, and were greeted by thousands of local fans who staged a riotous demonstration in the city streets in a long parade," according to the April 5, 1934, edition of the *Laramie Republican-Boomerang*.

It wasn't until 1936, when the stars from the first great Wyoming team were graduated and either playing AAU ball or just trying to survive the Great Depression, that the Helms Athletic Foundation was founded by Paul Helms and Bill Schroeder in Los Angeles. The organization put together a panel of experts to select national champion teams and make All-America selections in a number of sports, including football and basketball. The NCAA Tournament did not begin until 1939. The panel retroactively ranked football teams back to 1893 and basketball teams back to 1901. Wyoming was selected as the 1934 NCAA basketball national champions.

"I actually didn't realize that had happened," said Bob Hammond, the longtime sports editor of the *Laramie Daily Boomerang*, who wrote a column about the 1934 team in 2011. "It was a pretty bona fide thing. You look at it and the '34 season was fresh in their minds."

An argument was made that Kansas, which was 16-1 during the 1933-34 season, should have been named the national champion. The Jayhawks' only blemish was a 24-21 loss to Nebraska, a defeat they later avenged with a 25-24 win over the Cornhuskers. Wyoming beat Nebraska 33-24 on Jan. 20, 1934, in Lincoln. Kansas fans thought Wyoming had lost to the University of Tulsa, a weak college team that had a 6-8 record. Nearly 80 years later, the Wyoming basketball media guides still list the opponent for the Cowboys' March 18, 1934, loss simply as "Tulsa." The defeat was actually against the Diamond X Oilers of Tulsa, a semi-professional team comprised of older, more experienced players. Ironically, Kansas – one of the most storied program's in the game's history – has its Helms Foundation national championship banners from 1922 and 1923 hanging in historic Allen Fieldhouse next to the NCAA championship banners from 1952, 1988 and 2008.

"We just had a plaque for it, and nobody ever really said much about it," McKinney said of Wyoming's 1934 title. "They were kind of the forgotten team; the ghost team; the shadow men of our basketball tradition. We don't know as much about who they were and exactly what they did as we do with a Fennis Dembo, a Kenny Sailors, or all of the other guys weaved through our tradition."

Perhaps fittingly, considering the state's mostly isolated and rural make up, the accomplishments of the Cowboys' 1933-34 hardwood heroes were described in the newspapers and the school annual as "Wyoming vs. the World."

The Father of Wyoming Basketball

Everett F. Shelton dressed for success. The Hall of Fame coach wore stylish suits, perfectly tailored down to the handkerchief in the breast pocket and the tightly knotted tie, while working the officials and inspiring his Cowboys from Hell's Half Acre Gym in Laramie to Madison Square Garden in New York City. He also knew how to roll up his sleeves and go to work. Shelton was at his best in his true business attire: White t-shirt, white shorts, accentuated with a watch on his wrist and a whistle around his neck. Practice made the Pokes nearly perfect in 1943 and consistently good enough to win eight conference championships with eight NCAA Tournament appearances during Shelton's 19 seasons at Wyoming.

"A real gentlemen," is how Keith Bloom, a standout guard for the Cowboys from 1947-50, describes Shelton. "Practices were tough, they extended you for sure. He could really get on you at times, yet there was a balance of praise. He didn't say a whole lot, but when he spoke, you sat up and listened."

Shelton was born on May 12, 1898, in Cunningham, Kansas, where he was a high school baseball, basketball and football star. After graduating in 1916, he served in the U.S. Marine Corps during World War I as a machine gun sergeant at the Battles of Chateau-Thierry and Belleau Wood in France. Shelton was an all-conference quarterback and captained the basketball team at Phillips University in Enid, Oklahoma. He later became the head baseball, basketball and football coach at his alma mater. After Shelton guided Phillips to a 48-29 record from 1923-26, he began coaching at the AAU level. Eventually, one of his best friends in the business, iconic Oklahoma A&M (now Oklahoma State) coach Henry Iba recommended Shelton for the job as coach of the Denver Safeway AAU team. At the time, the best basketball players in the country played on the AAU circuit. In his second season (1937-38) in Denver, the Safeway squad, which was led by All-Americans and Naismith Hall of Fame inductees Jack McCracken and Bob Gruenig, won the AAU national championship. Shelton then coached the Colorado Springs Antlers Hotel AAU team in 1938-39 before accepting an offer from Wyoming athletic director John Corbett to build his own championship program in Laramie.

"I knew he was considered a great coach in AAU ball," said Kenny Sailors, whose arrival as a freshman at Wyoming coincided with Shelton's first season at the University. "A lot of people today don't know what AAU ball was. They were the same players that played in the NBA, All-Americans that came out of college from all over the nation and played for these companies."

The Cowboys, led by Willie Rothman's 10.5 points per game, got off to a strong start in the 1939-40 season with three consecutive wins over Colorado Mines to open the slate. Things deteriorated from there, however, as Wyoming went just 1-6 on the road and finished 6-10 overall. Shelton quickly instilled toughness in his teams that would serve them well in the years to come as the Cowboys traveled from coast to coast chasing a national championship. Over the next three seasons, the Pokes went a combined 60-13 overall, with a 22-0 record at Hell's Half Acre Gym, a 34-11 record in true road games, and a 4-2 record on neutral courts.

"I remember Ev as a dapper dresser, very controlled . . . he had good discipline on his teams," said Jim Brandenburg, Wyoming's head coach from 1979-88, who competed against Shelton's Cowboys as a Colorado State player in the 1950s. "I thought at the time he had command of the situation, and the players were disciplined. They played for defense and for shooting percentage. He paid attention to all the little things that let you win."

Shelton is credited with developing the methodical five-man weave offense, known in the Skyline Conference as the "Wyoming Weave" or "Shelton Weave," which Sailors and the 1942-43 Cowboys ran to perfection. Every player was in constant motion, either setting screens or making cuts.

"There wasn't any defense for it back then," Sailors said. "There isn't now if you do it right."

After the Cowboys' amazing run to a Helms Foundation national title in 1933-34, head coach Willard Witte was unable to remain on top of the Rocky Mountain Athletic Conference standings, accruing a respectable but less dominant 53-37 overall record over his final five seasons on the bench. But he did find another superstar to replace his brother Les Witte. John Winterholler played at Wyoming from 1936-39 and is considered one of the most outstanding all-around athletes in the school's annals. The Lovell native earned all-conference honors for the Pokes in football and was named to *Sports Illustrated's* Silver Anniversary

All-American football team in 1964. He was also an all-conference center fielder for the Wyoming baseball team and competed on the track team as a sprinter. During the 1936-37 basketball season, Winterholler led the Pokes in scoring.

"The Cowboy campus has produced no athlete who has attained the Lovell youth's heights," longtime Cheyenne newspaper man Larry Birleffi wrote of Winterholler at the time. "He is the athlete's idea of an athlete and a coach's answer."

During World War II, Winterholler was most American's idea of a hero. Winterholler was captured at the Battle of Corregidor and was a Japanese prisoner of war for 34 months, subsequently becoming paralyzed. He was a recipient of the Silver Star and promoted to a full colonel, all by the age of 30. Later in life he captained a wheelchair basketball team. On Oct. 31, 1964, the University of Wyoming celebrated "Johnnie Winterholler Day."

Following the war, Keith Bloom stepped on campus and would become the third noteworthy, homegrown Wyoming athlete – joining Milward Simpson and Winterholler – to earn varsity letters in three separate sports for the Cowboys. After completing his military service in the Navy during World War II, Bloom was offered a basketball scholarship by Shelton. The coach and athletic director Glenn "Red" Jacoby also encouraged the former Powell High School star to play football and baseball.

"I was really privileged to play for two national Hall of Fame coaches, Ev Shelton and Bowden Wyatt," Bloom said. "I played tight end on Wyatt's first team in Laramie. He changed Wyoming football, that's for sure."

Shelton pulled double duty as Wyoming's head baseball coach in 1947 and 1949, posting a 16-12 record in his two seasons in the dugout. Glenn "Bud" Daniel, a freshman catcher at Wyoming in 1941, returned after the war and played for Shelton.

"Ev would not let me catch batting practice when he was my coach. He said, 'You can hit all you want, but you're not going to catch. I need you on Friday and Saturday,'" said Daniel, who coached the Wyoming baseball program from 1951-71 and guided the Cowboys to their only College World Series appearance in 1956. "So Ev, who was in his mid-fifties at the time, caught batting practice everyday. He was black and blue all over."

Bloom hadn't played organized baseball, which isn't a sanctioned high school sport in Wyoming, growing up in Park County. Shelton was a great evaluator of talent and saw some potential in Bloom, perhaps the greatest athlete Powell has ever produced.

Bloom started at first base for three seasons, leading the team in putouts and fielding percentage as a junior and senior.

"Ev was coaching the baseball team, too, so he recruited (Loy) Doty and me from the basketball team. We didn't even have a legion team in Powell. I never played," Bloom said. "But Ev said, 'Well, you'd be a good first baseman.' I ended up lettering and played in the Utah Industrial League and one summer with the Worland (Wyoming) Indians. We won the Montana-Wyoming championship and qualified for the national semi-pro tournament in Wichita. The Coors Brewery team beat us 6-5 in 10 innings in the semifinals."

Wyatt, a member of the College Football Hall of Fame, produced a 39-17-1 record at Wyoming, including a perfect season (10-0) and a Gator Bowl victory in 1950. He left after the 1952 season to coach Arkansas and eventually built Tennessee, his alma mater, into a powerhouse.

"I was out for track my freshman year when Bowden started practicing spring football. I had enjoyed high school football and was one of 11 tailbacks trying out," Bloom recalled. "Two of the tailbacks were Earl 'Shadow' Ray and (James) O'Brien. Bowden said, 'How'd you like to be an end?'"

Bloom's career on the gridiron ended during a 21-6 loss at Colorado on Nov. 15, 1947, when he tore up a shoulder.

"Ev called me in and said, 'Red and I gave you a chance to play football and you did. But we're going to be ranked as one of top teams in the country and you better concentrate on basketball,'" Bloom said. "Ev provided the scholarship. I had no choice at that point."

After Sailors returned from World War II and completed his eligibility in 1946, Shelton was able to reload with Bloom and another great group of native Cowboys. The next big star of the program would be John Pilch, a 6-4 post player from Thermopolis, Wyoming, who earned All-American honors in 1950 and went on to play briefly for the Minneapolis Lakers. He led Wyoming in scoring for three consecutive seasons (1948-50), but Shelton was more impressed with Pilch's work in the paint, describing him as the greatest offensive and defensive rebounder he had ever coached.

"Pilch was an animal. He really was," Bloom said. "He wasn't all that big, but he sure was tough on the post and he had a great hook shot. John would put his elbow right in the defensive player's face and there was nothing they could do to stop that shot. I enjoyed getting the ball into John, because I knew some good things would happen."

The Pokes opened the 1946-47 season with seven consecutive wins, including a sweep of Washington State, before losing to UCLA at a tournament in Buffalo, New York. Two nights later, Wyoming lost 57-48 to CCNY at Madison Square Garden. The game stories focused on a benches-clearing brawl. The Cowboys were tearing up infamous coach Nat Holman's defense in the first half with the five-man weave. In the second half, however, the officials started blowing the whistles and calling illegal screen fouls on Wyoming. According to Bloom, who was sitting next to the coach on the bench, Shelton crossed the line verbally with a rant about the CCNY players directed at the officials. The offensive language echoed through Madison Square Garden and a physical confrontation between the teams ensued.

"Nat Holman left his bench and pointed a finger at Ev. Shortly after that, Jim Collins got a rebound and one of the CCNY players fell over Jimmy's shoulder, and the fists started flying," Bloom said. "It didn't last all that long, the blue coats came out and ushered us back to the bench. We finished the game with police standing behind each bench . . . . Holman told Ev, 'Well, you'll never be in the Garden again.' The *New York Times* story said, 'Wyoming banned from the Garden.' But Ned Irish, who managed the Garden at that time, said to Ev, 'You're welcome anytime. You're a great crowd pleaser.'

"We had a great time there and saw a lot of New York. Those trips seeing the country by rail were spectacular."

Wyoming dropped its third consecutive game on the East Coast trip, a 51-44 defeat at Temple on Jan. 1, 1947, before beating Holy Cross and Valparaiso at a tournament in Cleveland. The Pokes set the tone for the Skyline Conference season with a 60-30 thrashing of Colorado State. The regular season ended in similar fashion with a 52-38 victory in Fort Collins. It was the third conference championship for Jimmie Reese, Lou Roney and Floyd Volker, members of the 1943 national title team who had returned to the program after the war.

The March magic did not shine on the Pokes this time. Wyoming, which had eliminated Texas en route to Madison Square Garden four years earlier, lost in stunning fashion to the Longhorns in the first round of the NCAA Tournament in Kansas

City. The Cowboys had a 40-39 lead before turning the ball over and allowing Texas to steal the game, 42-40, in the final minute.

"That was terrible. We were right in the game all the way, and Slater Martin hit a running shot from the mid-court line and off the backboard," Bloom said. "That was the victory for them. That was hard to swallow."

Martin, a Naismith Hall of Fame inductee, went on to play in seven NBA All-Star Games during the 1950s, collecting four championships with the Minneapolis Lakers and another with the St. Louis Hawks. Texas advanced and ended up beating CCNY in the third-place game at the Final Four in New York. Wyoming, which had the distinction of beating the NCAA champions (Holy Cross) and NIT champions (Utah) that season, was drubbed by Oregon State in a consolation game the day after losing to the Longhorns, finishing the season with a 22-6 overall record.

The 1947-48 Wyoming team captured Shelton's fourth Skyline Conference trophy with road wins at Utah State (39-27) and Utah (41-37). Despite getting 20 points from Mark Peyton and 11 points from Doty, the Cowboys lost 58-48 to Kansas State in the first round of the NCAA Tournament on March 19, 1948, at historic Municipal Auditorium. Washington beat the Pokes, 57-47, in the consolation game to give Wyoming a final record of 18-9.

With Bloom captaining the team and Pilch poised for a monster junior season, the 1948-49 Pokes were clearly the favorites to win the Skyline Conference again and represent the region at the NCAA Tournament. The Cowboys went 10-3 during non-conference play. The highlight was finishing 3-1 – splitting two games with Oregon State and sweeping Oregon – during a four-games-in-four-nights road trip through the Pacific Northwest. The team was headed back from a holiday tournament in Los Angeles when the "Blizzard of '49" besieged the Rocky Mountain West. The Cowboys' train back to Laramie ended up getting stuck in Green River for three days.

"We saw cattle standing against a fence line frozen. That really caught our eye," Bloom recalled. "The conductor came through and said, 'We don't know where we are.' Well, we were in the Green River yards, where nine trains were snowbound. Ev got on a snowplow and got to Laramie, and we were still stuck in Green River. We met everybody on all nine trains. By the time the weather was starting to clear, there was no bread or candles left in Green River."

While Shelton was back in Laramie drawing up the X's and O's for a key home stand with Utah and Brigham Young to open up the conference schedule, the Cowboys decided to scrimmage the Rice Owls, who were also stranded in Green River during the blizzard. Ironically, the two teams had played the previous season at a holiday tournament in Oklahoma City. Wyoming prevailed 58-43 in that encounter.

"We had a game there in the Green River High School gym, and it was filled up because there wasn't anything for anybody to do," Bloom said. "I remember them putting us on snowmobiles and taking us to the gym . . . . The great thing about that experience and all the travel we did was the people you build friendships and bonds with on those trips and with all the games and practices and everything."

The tight-knit Cowboys eventually made it home and beat Utah (42-38) and BYU (59-48 and 58-38) to open conference play 3-0. After sweeping Utah State to end the regular season, Wyoming had won its fifth Skyline title and was headed back to the NCAA Tournament for the third consecutive season. But it turned out to be another cruel experience for the Pokes, who suffered a controversial 40-39 overtime loss to Oklahoma State on March 18, 1949, in Kansas City. Pilch scored 13 points and Bloom added nine, but it wasn't enough as the other Cowboys benefited from a no-call in the final seconds.

"That was one of Hank Iba's teams and they had to pass 25 or 30 times before taking a shot. And they played really tough defense," Bloom said. "Loy Doty was taken across the scorer's table and no foul was called and they beat us in a close game."

Wyoming lost 61-48 to Arkansas in a consolation game the next day to bring a close to a great decade of basketball for the program that included four different All-Americans (Bill Strannigan in 1941, Sailors in 1942, '43 and '46, Milo Komenich in 1943 and Jim Weir in 1943), five Skyline Conference championships, five NCAA Tournament appearances and one national championship.

"I had the privilege of playing with some of those fellows from the '43 team when they returned from the service," Bloom said. "What's remarkable about that championship team, there were so many Wyoming kids on it. That was the beauty of it."

Led by Pilch and a resplendent sophomore from Thermopolis named George "Moe" Radovich, Wyoming finished the 1949-50 season with a 25-11 record. But the Pokes lost twice to BYU in

Provo on back-to-back nights (March 3 and 4), which allowed the Cougars to claim the conference crown and make an appearance in the NCAA Tournament. It was a similar story in 1950-51 when Wyoming finished 26-11 but dropped three of four games against BYU. The Cougars once again represented the conference in the now expanded 16-team NCAA Tournament. Fittingly, Wyoming's lone win over BYU that season was a 50-49 thriller at Hell's Half Acre Gym. With construction on a new venue nearly complete, the Pokes capped an unforgettable era in the old digs with an 82-61 thrashing of Denver to close the 1950-51 season and blowout wins over Montana State (84-54 and 82-54) to get the 1951-52 season off to a fast start.

Wyoming's final record at Hell's Half Acre from 1924-51 was 222-44, a winning percentage of .835, including spotless seasons in 1929, 1930, 1933, 1934, 1941, 1942, 1943 and 1947.

"The students lined up well ahead of the games at Half Acre, and it was just packed," Bloom said. "There wasn't an aisle open or anything, and they hung over that railing. It was fun to play in there. The fans were close and there were no barriers between them and the players. It was just a great atmosphere."

Construction on War Memorial Fieldhouse and War Memorial Stadium went on simultaneously, so the exact cost of each project is not known. But the estimated bill for the 69,680 square foot basketball facility, which at the time was the largest building in the state, is $1 million. The state-of-the-art removable court, which was raised 16 inches off the tanbark arena floor, had a price tag of $20,000. Shelton's boys broke their new home in with a 78-69 victory over St. Mary's on Dec. 14, 1951, and lost a nail-biter to Indiana, 57-55, the next night. Rival Colorado State played the same two teams at War Memorial Fieldhouse that weekend.

"When that was built it was the palace of basketball venues in the Rocky Mountain region. That thing was really something," said longtime "Laramie Boomerang" sports Editor Bob Hammond. "I remember going to the games as a kid, and it had a uniqueness about it with the raised floor and the tanbark all the way around it. They used to wet the tanbark down, and when you're a kid and you smell that and everything, it was pretty cool going in there and running around."

Wyoming also beat Baylor at War Memorial Fieldhouse, picked up a road win at Oregon, and beat Alabama on a neutral court at a tournament during non-conference play. Even sweeter for the Pokes was a sweep of BYU on the way to the Skyline

Conference title. Shelton won his first NCAA Tournament game since 1943 with Wyoming's 54-48 victory over Oklahoma City on March 21, 1952, in Corvallis, Ore. Radovich scored 13 points, and Ron Rivers added 11. The Cowboys' memorable season ended with a 56-53 loss to Santa Clara the next evening. Radovich, the two-time Skyline Conference Player of the Year, earned UPI All-American honors as a senior. He played professionally for the Philadelphia Warriors before entering the Army.

With players like Bill Sharp, Harry Jorgensen, Ron Rivers and Jim Mulvehal leading the way, Wyoming captured its seventh Skyline Conference championship in 1952-53. The Cowboys won nine of their first 10 conference games and wrapped up the regular season with a 54-53 victory against the Rams in Fort Collins. Santa Clara ended the run with a 67-52 victory over Wyoming in the first round of the expanded 22-team NCAA Tournament on March 13, 1953. The Pokes were pounded by Seattle, 80-64, in a consolation game the next day. The Cowboys went 19-9 in 1953-54 and 17-9 in 1954-55, but the conference was won by Colorado State (coached by the ex-Poke star Strannigan) in 1954 and Utah in 1955. Shelton's final four seasons at Wyoming ended with losing records.

When Tony Windis was growing up in Long Island, New York, he remembers going to Madison Square Garden and watching the Providence Steamrollers play the New York Knicks. Two of the Providence standouts, Kenny Sailors and George Nostrand, had been collegiate stars at Wyoming. Sailors, of course, led the Cowboys to the NCAA championship on the same floor in 1943. Nostrand, a 6-8 power forward/center, only lettered one season (1945) at Wyoming as the 1943-44 season was quashed due to World War II. Windis never dreamed he would follow in their footsteps and play for Shelton in Laramie. In fact, the future scoring machine didn't even play that much basketball in high school. Windis' coach hid him on the bench as a freshman and only practiced him as a sophomore. When the quiet young man with the pure jump shot finally got his chance, Windis helped lead the High School of Commerce to the New York City championship in 1950.

"Even my junior year, I didn't play very much until January when our best player signed a contract to play baseball with the

Brooklyn Dodgers," Windis said. "And then we went on and won the city-wide championship. I was honorable mention all-city, including all five boroughs. I was ready to play some more ball."

Windis' senior season was canceled due to a teachers' strike. He spent the next two years in the Army and was playing in a basketball game in France when someone from Wyoming saw him play and provided Shelton with an intriguing scouting report. When Windis returned home to New York from the service, a letter from Shelton was waiting. The legendary coach was offering him a scholarship to play basketball for the Cowboys. Windis, much to the surprise of his parents, who didn't realize at the time exactly how far Laramie was from Long Island, wrote Shelton back accepting the offer.

"I went on a date to the movies with a girl. We saw Jimmy Stewart in 'The Man from Laramie,'" Windis recalled. "And I told her, 'You know, I've got a chance to go to Laramie.'

"She said I was full of baloney."

The city kid was serious about playing college basketball in rural Wyoming. He had worked on a farm in upstate New York as a boy and fell in love with the wide open spaces.

"I like elbow room," said Windis, who still lives in Rawlins, Wyoming.

Wyoming had finished 7-19 during the 1955-56 season, despite the presence of scoring machine Joe Capua. The wiry, 5-10 guard from Gary, Indiana, who reminded many old Pokes fans of Sailors, averaged 24.5 points that year as a senior. He scored 637 points in 26 games to set a new program single-season record; Milo Komenich owned the previous mark with 551 points in 33 games (16.7 per) during the Cowboys' national title run. On Feb. 3, 1956, Capua tallied 51 points during a 93-69 victory over Montana, which remains Wyoming's single-game scoring record to this day. He made 16 field goals and 19 free throws. Had the 3-point line been in existence and had he not missed seven free throws, the record might be closer to 70 points. Two nights later, Capua tallied 32 points in a win over Utah to complete the greatest back-to-back scoring statistics produced in the program's proud history.

"One of my first real memories of Wyoming basketball, other than just going to the games, was the night that Joe Capua scored 51 points," Hammond said. "I was just a kid then. Back then at the old Fieldhouse, if the ball went off the floor it would go into the orchestra pit or way, way down off the raised court. So they would have a football player on each end sit in a chair with a basketball. If the basketball went off the floor, they would quickly throw one to the ref and went and got the other ball. I was right up there with that football player on my hands and knees, right up by the floor watching the game that night."

Capua was an All-Skyline selection as a junior and senior and was named to UPI's "little man's" All-American first team and to the Helms All-American first team.

"He was a very good ball player," Windis said. "During my freshman year, I had to write everything down in the score books and chart the shots for Shelton."

Windis said the coach still ran a "slow-down" offense during his twilight Laramie days. The trend in the late 1950s for Shelton was an ability to recruit and turn loose scoring stars. Meanwhile, Wyoming continued to slip in the conference standings.

During the 1956-57 season, Windis exploded onto the Skyline Conference scene, averaging a team-high 19.0 points per game as a sophomore.

"I used to go up in the driveway and pretend I was Tony Windis," Hammond said. "He had a two-hand, behind-the-head shot. It was the craziest shot I've ever seen, but it was productive."

The Pokes played a difficult schedule, as Shelton always did, but never recovered from a 0-6 start against the likes of Oregon State, Southern California and Oklahoma State. Wyoming finished the season 6-19, including a 3-8 record at War Memorial Fieldhouse. Shelton was starting to feel the heat because the program was not living up to the lofty standards he had established on the high plains.

"I felt sorry for Ev because everyone was on his back," Windis said.

Wyoming stumbled out of the gate again in 1957-58 with a 1-6 start – that included road games at Wichita State, Nebraska, Oklahoma City, Oklahoma State and Tulsa – before regrouping with wins over Michigan and Wisconsin from the Big Ten at a holiday tournament in Albuquerque, New Mexico. On Jan. 10, 1958, the Cowboys beat New Mexico 101-61 to get the Skyline Conference season off to an impressive beginning, but that wasn't the head- line from the game. Windis put 50 points on the Lobos that night at War Memorial Fieldhouse. He had a chance to break

Capua's single-game scoring record, but some shots he could normally make in his sleep rimmed out late in the lopsided contest.

"Everything went well. Everything I threw up seemed to go in, except at the very end I had two layups that I missed," Windis said. "Basketball is a funny game."

Windis averaged 20.9 points during his junior season and led Wyoming to its eighth Skyline Conference title and eighth NCAA Tournament appearance under Shelton. The Pokes finished the season just 13-14 overall, but sewed up their much-needed postseason berth with a four-game winning streak against New Mexico, BYU, Utah State and Colorado State late in the season. Unfortunately for the Cowboys, their first-round draw was Elgin Baylor-led Seattle. Wyoming was drubbed 88-51 by the eventual national runner-up squad on March 12, 1958, in Berkeley, California Windis was held in check as John Bertolero (22 points) and Donald Hatten (12 points) led the Cowboys in scoring. Baylor finished with 26 points and was named the Most Outstanding Player of the 24-team tournament, despite Seattle's 84-72 loss to Kentucky in the national championship.

"Seattle beat us pretty convincingly," Windis recalled 53 years later. "They had Elgin Baylor, and we learned a lesson."

It would be Windis' only appearance in the NCAA Tournament and the 16th and final game Shelton would coach in the Big Dance. Windis continued to shred Skyline Conference defenses as a senior, averaging 24.3 points per game and finishing a brilliant collegiate career with 1,465 points. But Wyoming finished the unmerciful 1958-59 campaign with a 4-22 record. Windis moved on to a brief NBA career with the Detroit Pistons before returning to Wyoming and becoming the first high school coach in state history to lead both a boys and girls team (Mountain View High School) to state championships in the same year.

"I had a bunch of good girls and boys. My coaching success is more or less blended on three simple things – simplicity, discipline and respect," said Windis, who occasionally has coffee with Sailors in Laramie. "That's all I did. I venture to say it worked out for me. And Shelton told me that if I was crazy enough to coach that those are the principles to use."

Shelton left Wyoming after losing 15 of his final 16 games down the stretch over the long winter of 1959. He went on to coach at Sacramento State, where he had a 188-188 record and led the program to the Division II (known as the College Division

Tournament) national championship game – a classic 58-57 double-overtime loss to Mount St. Mary's – in 1962. Shelton's Hall of Fame career, which spanned 46 seasons and included over 800 wins, came to an end in 1968. On April 16, 1974, Windis phoned his college coach. Shelton's wife broke the bad news to him.

"I tried to call him on the same day that he died," Windis said. "He was my coach and he taught me a lot."

Shelton was enshrined in the Naismith Memorial Basketball Hall of Fame posthumously in 1980. Wyoming's victory over Georgetown in the NCAA championship on March 30, 1943, followed by the overtime conquest over NIT champion St. John's on April 1, 1943, had already immortalized the coach and his Cowboys in college basketball lore. This sentiment was captured succinctly in the United Press International account of the Cowboys' legendary run at Madison Square Garden, written by Jack Cuddy for the April 2, 1943, editions.

This quintet operate from a campus in Laramie that has an altitude of 7,200 feet – an altitude which gives most visitors a nose bleed. Afterwards, the Wyoming coach – bespectacled Everett Shelton – admitted that the Wyoming triumph was due largely to altitude, not to the heights that could be measured by engineers, but rather to the heights attained psychologically by a team that was determined to win.

Strannigan and the Soaring '60s

Kevin McKinney has probably witnessed more Wyoming basketball games than anyone. The veteran sports information director and current associate athletic director has worked at the school for over 40 years and served as the color man on radio broadcasts for nearly 30 years. He was court-side calling the Cowboys' victory over UCLA on the way to the Sweet 16 in 1987, and the 57-56 win over Utah in 2002 that delivered the program's last outright conference title and NCAA Tournament appearance. Those two moments rank at or near the top of McKinney's list of professional highlights. However, his love affair with the program and fondest memories of the Cowboys were developed as an impressionable young fan in the 1960s. McKinney grew up in Cheyenne and frequently made the treacherous dead-of-winter drive over to Laramie for games as a kid. During those trips he sat in the back seat of the car as his father, John, the engineer of the radio broadcasts, and Hall of Fame sports writer and broadcaster Larry Birleffi discussed all things Pokes.

McKinney's office – decorated with photographs of Wyoming hoops heroes such as Fennis Dembo and Reggie Slater, and visited frequently by living legend Kenny Sailors – is located down the hall from War Memorial Fieldhouse. McKinney still remembers the first time he walked into the old basketball barn to watch Pokes play. The date was Dec. 19, 1959, and the Cowboys lost 82-78 to Michigan State.

"It was just such a thrill for me," McKinney recalled. "I'd always gone to Story Gymnasium because I loved watching the Cheyenne High School games. Dad and Larry did those, too. But when they brought me over, the Fieldhouse was so incredibly huge to me. They did the game from the press box in those days, and I sat right underneath. It wasn't a full house by any means. I watched everything that was going on and I was so overwhelmed. I'll never forget it. Little did I know I'd work in that press box and be here all this time. Were we any good?"

McKinney opens an old media guide to answer his own question. No, the Cowboys were not any good. Quite the opposite. The 1959-60 season was Bill Strannigan's first as head coach at his alma mater. Wyoming, which had a three-game winning streak entering the marquee non-conference matchup with the Spartans from the Big Ten, finished 5-19.

"Some of Bill's teams were horrible," McKinney concedes. "It's funny because the era you grow up in is usually the golden years. Those guys . . . that's how I grew up with basketball. The pros were scoring 150, and the Cowboys were scoring 100. That's the way basketball was. Defense? Forget it. We went to see Flynn Robinson take that patented shot. We all tried it, we all worked on it. Flynn, Randy Richardson, Leon Clark, Reuben Poindexter, Harry Hall . . . those guys ran the floor, scored the ball, and played little defense."

McKinney's favorite game from the era was on Jan. 15, 1966, when Wyoming beat Brigham Young University 107-101. The Cougars averaged 95.5 points that season, ascended to number 1 in the national polls, and won the NIT at Madison Square Garden. Many of the BYU standouts from that great Western Athletic Conference (WAC) team – Jeff Congdon, Dick Nemelka, Craig Raymond, Neil Roberts – attended the program's final Mountain West home game, a 102-78 victory over the Cowboys on March 5, 2011, in Provo, Utah.

"That era of Wyoming basketball . . . they didn't have great records, but it was so exciting," McKinney said. "It was basketball the way I think it should be played . . . . Fennis and Eric (Leckner), that era was fun, but they were the kids, and I was here a long time. It still means everything to me, but it wasn't the same as seeing Leon Clark dunk."

With BYU leaving its old rivals behind to become independent in football and join the West Coast Conference in other sports, and Utah becoming a member of the Pac-12, Wyoming's only true Mountain West rival that dates back to the glory days of Sailors and the 1943 team is Colorado State. Despite the lack of love between the Cowboys and Rams, the effervescent Strannigan was able to coach on both sides of the Border War. "Billy the Kid" grew up in Rock Springs, earned All-American honors for the Pokes on the basketball court, ran the single wing as a tailback on the football field, and was the ace pitcher on the baseball team during a remarkable playing career at Wyoming from 1940-42. After graduating, Strannigan played for the Denver American Legion team where he won an AAU national championship and earned All-American honors. When Strannigan's playing days ended, he began coaching. His first head coaching opportunity happened to be at CSU, where he went 1-9 head-to-head against Ev Shelton and the Cowboys. In his fourth season (1953-54) in Fort Collins, Strannigan guided the Rams to a 22-7 record and the program's first NCAA Tournament appearance.

"It is unique," Jim Brandenburg, a former CSU player who became one of Wyoming's great head coaches, said of being on both sides of the rivalry. "The thing about Bill Strannigan is he was a hell of a football player and a hell of a basketball player."

Strannigan left CSU for Iowa State, where he compiled a 70-45 record from 1955-59. During his brief but memorable time in Ames, the Cyclones garnered their first-ever national ranking with an 18-5 finish to the 1955-56 season. Strannigan's team produced arguably the greatest win in program history, a 39-37 victory over top-ranked Kansas, which featured Wilt Chamberlain, on Jan. 14, 1957. After the 1959 season, Strannigan decided to leave Iowa State for the challenge of replacing his mentor, Shelton, at Wyoming. Rebuilding the program at his alma mater proved to be a difficult task as Strannigan went 46-73 over his first five seasons back in Laramie. But the excitement level and athleticism at War Memorial Fieldhouse would reach new heights with the arrival of some of the greatest athletes Wyoming fans have ever cheered for.

Most basketball fans remember Flynn James Robinson as an accomplished NBA player. The sleek, 6-foot-1 guard was selected by the Cincinnati Royals in the 1965 draft, where he played with Oscar Robinson and Jerry Lucas.

"One thing that got me better was Lucas was a workaholic. I used to spend an hour before and after every practice shooting with him," Robinson said. "It makes your confidence better. Basketball is a game of confidence. Playing against Oscar in practice was a treat because he was one of the greatest players of all time."

Flynn Robinson also played for the Chicago Bulls, Milwaukee Bucks and Baltimore Bullets during his NBA career, as well as one season with the San Diego Conquistadors of the ABA. He appeared in the 1970 NBA All-Star Game on the East team along with Bucks teammate Kareem Abdul-Jabbar. But his best seasons were spent in Los Angeles with the Lakers, running amongst a lineup of legends that included Chamberlain and Jerry

West. The 1971-72 Lakers won 69 games, including an NBA-record 33 straight, on the way to the franchise's first championship. Robinson, who was nicknamed "Instant Offense" by famous Lakers broadcaster Chick Hearn, was the team's top scorer coming off the bench behind West and Gail Goodrich.

"Scoring is something that I've been doing all my life," said Robinson, now 70, who was still playing in runs at the Westchester (California) YMCA and in senior tournaments around the country well into his 60s.

Greater Chicago is a basketball hot bed that has produced some of the most dynamic players in Wyoming history. Elgin, Illinois, located about 40 miles northwest of The Windy City, is almost as bitterly cold in the winter as Laramie. Robinson, after initially enrolling at Southern Illinois out of high school, played at Casper College for one season before becoming an All-American at Wyoming.

"The rest is history," Robinson said.

Robinson averaged 26.2 points during his first season (1962-63), 25.6 points per game as a junior (1963-64), and a school-record 27.0 points per game as a senior (1964-65). His career scoring average (26.3 ppg) is easily the highest in Cowboys history (Tony Windis is second on the list at 21.2 points per game). And despite playing for only three seasons, Robinson is second in career points scored (2,049) behind Dembo (2,311), who awed fans for four unforgettable seasons in the late 1980s while benefiting from a 3-point line that was not in existence during the high-scoring 1960s.

During a post-Christmas tournament in Oklahoma City, Dec. 26-29, 1962, the Robinson-led Cowboys upset Creighton 80-74 in the opening round. The Jays' star, future NBA player and head coach Paul Silas, averaged an astonishing 20.6 rebounds per game that season. Wyoming edged host Oklahoma City (65-64) the next night before losing to Loyola (Illinois) 93-82 in the championship game.

"That kind of got Wyoming basketball stirred up again," Robinson recalled.

The Cowboys finished 11-15 in 1963 and 12-14 in 1964, but Strannigan put together brutal non-conference challenges that included road trips to California, Kansas, Oregon, Stanford, Washington and Wichita State.

"We had a tough schedule all three years. We could have had an easier schedule, but coach Strannigan wanted to play good teams," Robinson said. "And I'm so happy he did, because it gave me a better opportunity when I got drafted by Cincinnati. I fell right into place in the NBA because we had played such good teams and players when I was at Wyoming. Coach Strannigan and (assistant) Moe Radovich treated us good and made us better . . . .

"Strannigan was like a dad to me. He got me down there and taught me a lot," Robinson said. "And he kind of built the team around me a little bit."

On Feb. 13, 1965, Robinson scored 40 points to lead Wyoming to a 111-102 victory over Utah in Laramie.

"I was in school at the same time Flynn was, and that was back when Muhammad Ali was really a big thing," said Bob Hammond, the deep-rooted sports editor of the Laramie Boomerang. "I gave him a ride from class up to the Union one day, and it was snowing. Wyoming was going to play Utah. I said, 'Flynn, how many are you going to get this week?' He said, 'I don't know, never can tell . . . with Utah, they break my spell.'"

Robinson scored 48 points during an 89-80 loss at Arizona State on Feb. 22, 1964, which remains a Wyoming single-game road scoring record. The Sun Devils were led by "Jumpin'" Joe Caldwell, the second overall pick in the 1964 NBA Draft and a member of the U.S. Olympic team that captured the gold medal in Tokyo. Bill Purden, a Wyoming assistant responsible for recruiting a number of star players to the high plains of Laramie from urban Illinois during the 1960s, was good friends with Arizona State head coach Ned Wulk, who informed him after the fact that Caldwell had requested to guard Robinson that evening.

"Wulk was telling Bill, the first two or three times down the floor Flynn hits what would have been long 3-point shots today," Hammond said. "Wulk calls a timeout and Caldwell says, 'Coach, put somebody else on him.'"

The 1964-65 Cowboys produced Strannigan's much-needed first winning season (16-10) at Wyoming. Robinson finished the season with 701 points in 26 games. Wyoming capped off the campaign with a 107-102 victory over Utah in Salt Lake City to sweep the Utes.

"The Flynn era was my favorite because I was very impressionable. I was growing up, and we all tried to be Flynn," McKinney said. "Everybody tried to shoot like Flynn. He was our hero, he was the guy. There was no television, but we listened to Larry (Birleffi) call the games as Flynn would score 48, or whatever he had, at Arizona State."

Robinson became the 20th player to score over 2,000 points in a college career with 2,049 points in three seasons at Wyoming. He led the WAC in scoring and was named a Helms Foundation All-American all three years. The longtime Los Angeles resident has had a chance to visit with a number of Wyoming's other NBA players – Leckner, Reggie Slater, Theo Ratliff – over the years, and Robinson even watched a Cowgirls game with Sailors during a trip back to Laramie.

"For a guy from a little college, I would say I achieved quite a bit," said Robinson, who recently survived a battle with cancer that required the removal of a brain tumor. "Wyoming is a beautiful state. I used to go up to Centennial, and it's breathtaking for a person who has never been out there . . . . I'm just proud to have gone there. The people have always treated me great. If you're a good individual and work hard, the people of Wyoming will support you."

Robinson's departure for the NBA allowed several other worthy Wyoming players to step into the spotlight at War Memorial Fieldhouse in the years that followed, starting with Clark and Dick Sherman. They starred for the Cowboys during a 17-9 finish in 1965-66. One of the highlights was a 99-92 victory over St. Joseph's (Pennsylvania), which was ranked in the top five at the time, coached by Jack Ramsey and led by future NBA standout Matt Goukas. The Cowboys were 8-1 at home in WAC play but 3-5 on the road, including key late-season losses to conference champion CSU and rivals BYU and Utah. Sherman, one of the greatest athletes Cheyenne has ever produced, led Wyoming in field-goal percentage for the third consecutive season and averaged 21.2 points and 10.2 rebounds a game as a senior.

"Strannigan was probably the best offensive-minded coach I've ever met. He just knew how to score a lot of points," Sherman said. "We pressed all the time and ran all the time. If they had a shot clock back then we would never have come close to using all of it. Our biggest problem was we weren't a real tall team."

Clark, listed at 6-6, was the team's center and a three-time All-WAC selection who finished his collegiate career with 1,497 points and 889 rebounds in 78 games. He grabbed 24 boards against Arizona State on March 5, 1966, and his 11.4 rebounds-per-game average remains a school record. Clark was a second-round pick of the Boston Celtics but never played in an NBA game and died in the mid-1970s from a heart attack.

"He was great. Good rebounder, good defensive ball player," Sherman said. "The only problem was Clark never passed me the ball. Neither did Flynn."

Despite Strannigan's fast-break style – Wyoming averaged 91 points a game during the 1964-65 season – it could be difficult for other players to get the shots they felt they deserved running alongside Robinson and Clark. But on Dec. 27, 1965, Sherman dropped 44 points on Rhode Island during a 107-101 loss at the annual holiday tournament in Oklahoma City. Imagine the numbers the Pokes would have put on the scoreboard during this era if the 3-point line had existed.

"That would have been outstanding for myself and Flynn because we were outside shooters. I got 44 one night, and I could have had 60," Sherman said. "Flynn was trying to make it into the NBA and trying to score as many as he could. Sometimes he hurt us more than helped us, but he was a great shooter."

Both Colorado State and Utah made the 22-team NCAA Tournament in 1966. Wyoming split with the Rams but suffered two deflating defeats against the Utes, a 93-91 overtime loss in Laramie and a 107-103 loss in Salt Lake City.

Sherman graduated from Wyoming in 1966. He was selected as the most outstanding education major and most distinguished military graduate for the school's ROTC program. A helicopter pilot in Vietnam, Sherman earned the Distinguished Flying Cross for heroism during a 31-year career in the Army.

"It was fun," Sherman said of what it is like for a Wyoming native to play for the Cowboys at a high level. "The Fieldhouse was like an old cow barn, basically. It seated 9,000, and when they filled it up it was rocking and rolling. My parents never missed a game. Cheyenne really supported the Cowboys in those days."

Stan Dodds grew up in the speck-on-a-map town of Granger, Wyoming, and bussed to Green River for high school. He quickly developed into a local basketball star recruited by Air Force, BYU, Colorado State and even Memphis State. Dodds was an admirer of Jerry Hill, the seemingly mythical kid from Torrington, Wyoming, who tore up defenses while leading the Wyoming football team to a victory in the 1958 Sun Bowl en route to a storied career with the Baltimore Colts that included an NFL championship in 1958 and a victory in Super Bowl V.

"I did want to stay at home, in a sense. There weren't a lot of athletes that were able to represent the University from our state. What I wanted to do was follow the steps of Jerry Hill," Dodds said. "I thought, 'Wouldn't that be neat to be from Wyoming and get to that level?' Coach Strannigan did a great job recruiting me. He was the speaker at our state championship banquet after my junior year."

When Dodds started high school, he was 5-9. When he graduated, he was 6-3. He grew another inch and a half at Wyoming. Strannigan, after getting players like Robinson and Clark to come play at 7,220 feet, had a good reputation as a recruiter, but not as a disciplinarian. During Dodds' freshman season (1966-67), the coach changed that perception by booting another potential star player, Ken Collins, off the team for not conforming to his rules.

"Strannigan was a great coach. He had high expectations and he didn't want anyone horsing around," Dodds said. "When he kicked an athlete like Ken out of the program, it sure got all of our attention. We knew we had to do things right and follow his guidelines."

The Cowboys struggled with consistency that season, but the roster still had plenty of talent with noteworthy players like Carl Ashley, Harry Hall, Mike Eberle, Bob Wilson and Tom Asbury. After starting the season 6-10, including a deflating home loss to Air Force, Wyoming rallied to win eight of its final nine WAC games and tied BYU for the regular-season title. The surging Cowboys then beat the Cougars 70-63 at Salt Lake City, a "neutral site" playoff game, to advance to the NCAA Tournament for the first time in nine years. The Pokes reward was a first-round matchup against All-American center Lew Alcindor and John Wooden's top-ranked UCLA Bruins.

"UCLA crushed us," Asbury recalled in the Denver Post. "The season was still memorable."

Asbury scored 20 points and Hall added 19 against UCLA, which pummeled Wyoming 109-60 on March 17, 1967, in Berkeley, California The Bruins went on to win the first of seven consecutive NCAA titles. Alcindor scored 29 points on the Cowboys and won the first of his three Most Outstanding Player awards that March. After the game, Alcindor even posed for photos with some of the Wyoming players, including one with Eberle that can be found at the Brown 'N Gold store on Grand Avenue in Laramie. Wyoming lost a consolation game to UTEP, 69-67, the next day.

The 1967-68 season began with the Cowboys averaging 101.6 points per game during a 5-0 start against lesser opponents. At times, however, including against BYU, UCLA and UTEP during the previous post season, Strannigan decided to run a slow-down offense dubbed the "Strannigan Shuffle." The Pokes, after thrilling wins over USC (79-78) and Iowa State (94-87, double overtime), were unable to slow down UCLA during the Bruins' holiday tournament in Los Angeles, losing the rematch 104-71 on Dec. 30, 1967.

"We started out the first half and thought it was fantastic," Dodds recalled. "Coach Strannigan called timeout with five minutes to go before halftime and said, 'You guys are right with them, we're only down two.' Before half we were down 15."

Dodds was the Cowboys' leading scorer at UCLA and was feeling good about the start of his sophomore season until running into Willie Long and New Mexico, who used a 1-3-1 zone trap against Wyoming's latest pure-shooting weapon. The Lobos prevailed 81-65.

"After my success, or what I thought was success at UCLA, we went over there and the papers wrote me and Ashley up as sophomores," Dodds said. "I didn't score a point. It really put me in a state where I needed to reflect immensely. Strannigan knew who he could get on or who to pamper. He said, 'I don't know if Stan Dodds is ready for the WAC Conference.' I thought, 'Boy, am I going to have to prove something to him.' He knew how to get to each player, and that's why he became such a great coach."

Wyoming finished the regular season 18-8 overall and 9-5 in the WAC, but settled for a trip to the NIT where the Cowboys lost 77-66 to Villanova, thanks to a 38-point scoring night by the Wildcats' Johnny Jones. Eberle scored 16 points to pace the Pokes. Dodds had suffered an ankle injury and was unable to play down the stretch.

In 1968-69, Wyoming opened the season with a 7-0 record, including wins over Stanford and Oklahoma. During the holiday tournament in Oklahoma City, the Cowboys suffered their first loss, 84-78 against "Pistol" Pete Maravich-led LSU. The Pokes won their final three WAC games – a 68-67 overtime victory at Arizona, followed by a home sweep of Utah (82-64) and BYU (79-69) – to tie for the conference title again and finish the regular season 18-7.

This time the Cougars prevailed 95-82 in a playoff at Phoenix. Wyoming headed back to New York City and lost 51-49 to Army. The Black Knights were coached by a young Bob Knight and led by a baby-faced point guard by the name of Mike Krzyzewski, in the NIT. Dodds led the Cowboys with 12 points and 10 rebounds in defeat.

"Just awesome," is how Dodds describes the feeling of playing in the old Madison Square Garden, where Wyoming captured the NCAA championship 26 years earlier. "You were just in awe when you stepped in there. It reminds you of Hoosiers. Especially me coming from Granger, Wyoming, it just felt like a massive coliseum to me. I'd never been in an arena with that type of seating, and of course the history behind it. It was like playing in heaven, and it was an honor to be there. They tore it down the next year."

Dodds was an All-WAC selection as a senior while leading the Cowboys in scoring at 20.7 points per game, while shooting 56 percent from the field. On Feb. 28, 1970, Dodds scored 45 points to lead Wyoming to a 112-94 victory over Arizona State at War Memorial Fieldhouse. He made 19 field goals that night, many from what would be 3-point distance in today's game.

"The Fieldhouse had the best floor around. I don't know that I played on a better floor, even at Madison Square Garden," Dodds said. "I look at that tape (from the Arizona State game), and I have 16 millimeter film from that night, I scored 45 on 19-of-31 field goals. I'd say probably 14 or 15 of them were outside what would be the arc. So I probably would have been close to 60 with a 3-point line."

The Pokes finished 19-7 in 1969-70, but were swept by WAC champion UTEP that year. It would be Strannigan's final winning season at Wyoming as the program went into a painful decline for the better part of a decade. Basketball would never quite feel the same for those who followed the Cowboys up close and personal during those free-flowing games at War Memorial Fieldhouse in the 1960s.

"Being down on the tanbark at the Fieldhouse when Flynn Robinson came out . . . it was rock star status," McKinney said. "That was a great time for me. I loved coming over and being in the Fieldhouse, I loved the raised floor and the scoreboard in the center of the floor. That was my era."

Black Pioneers Opened the Door

Curt Jimerson broke through racial barriers everywhere he went in life. The last place the talented high school All-American planned to make college basketball history was in Laramie.

"I was recruited by Arizona, Arizona State, New Mexico, Pepperdine," Jimerson said. "There was no way in hell I was going to Wyoming."

Jimerson grew up in El Paso, Texas, as the fourth of 10 children. His parents instilled a remarkable work ethic in their kids that served Jimerson well through the years. During high school, Jimerson's schedule was as follows: Wake up a 4:45 a.m. for a janitorial shift cleaning offices . . . band rehearsal at 7:15 a.m. . . . classes from 8 a.m. to 3:30 p.m. . . . basketball practice after school until at least 6 p.m. . . . walk home.

"Boy, that was tough. Sometimes I was so tired I couldn't even eat," Jimerson said. "But that's what my parents stressed. My parents pushed me a lot. My mom used to say all the time, 'I want you to have a better life than I had. The way to do it is to work hard and get an education.'"

Working hard is one thing. Fighting segregation at the same time takes a lot of courage and determination for a teenager. Jimerson was one of eight black students who first integrated El Paso's Austin High School. "I was prepared for anything after that," Jimerson said.

Jimerson played for two seasons at Pueblo (Colorado) Junior College and was an NJCCA All-American in 1959 after averaging 21.1 points per game. The success led to the mailbox full of scholarship offers. Texas Western (now called the University of Texas-El Paso or UTEP) was one of the schools where Jimerson had a chance to play Division I basketball. But his hometown program meant it a little too literally.

"I was very disappointed in Texas Western because they wanted me to stay at home and not in dorms," Jimerson said. "I told them I was one of 10 kids and there was nowhere for me to study at home. They said, 'Go to the library.'"

After looking at a poster of the pristine Colorado campus in Boulder, Jimerson decided to play for the Buffs and enjoy college life under the Flatirons. Colorado had already recruited black players, starting with Denver Manual High School star Billy Lewis, whose first varsity game was during the 1957-58 season. But one afternoon while studying in the office of legendary Pueblo Junior

College head coach Harry Simmons, Jimerson came across a letter from Colorado head coach Russell "Sox" Walseth about him.

"I opened it up and Sox Walseth was telling my coach that the boosters were upset because they were bringing in another black player," Jimerson said. "He told my coach that they already had 'two Negroes' starting, so he would leave me on the bench for the first three minutes and then put me in."

Jimerson decided not to attend Colorado. He never told Simmons or Walseth, who are now deceased, about reading the letter. After weighing all of his options, Jimerson decided to go to Wyoming because Bill Strannigan and his staff were the only ones willing to offer him a three-year scholarship. In 1960, Jimerson and Ron Bostick were believed to have been the first black basketball players at Wyoming. Jimerson, of course, was used to dealing with segregation and racism growing up in Texas. Bostick was from Saratoga Springs, New York, and was unaware of perceived lines he was crossing socially in small-town Laramie.

"Ron didn't see a problem dating white girls and he got called out by the athletic director," Jimerson said. "They called him in and told him to stop the relationship or his scholarship was gone. That's why Ron didn't come back. He was devastated."

Bostic left Wyoming after the 1960-61 season and graduated from California State University in San Jose. He served in the U.S. Air Force before successful careers in law enforcement and business. He died on April 13, 2009.

"There weren't many blacks in that school at all," Jimerson said. "There was definitely a wall."

If iconic athletic director Glenn "Red" Jacoby did give Bostick an ultimatum, his stance changed six years later when Mel Hamilton sat in the same office. The powerful Cowboys' offensive lineman was given Jacoby's blessing when he announced his intentions to marry a white co-ed. But that news did not sit well with Wyoming football coach Lloyd Eaton.

"Red Jacoby said, 'That's great Mel.' He thought it was a good idea to settle down," Hamilton said. "But Eaton said, 'Oh, hell no. I can't let you marry a white girl with the people of Wyoming's money.'"

Hamilton did not marry the girl and left the program to join the Army after helping the Cowboys to a 10-1 record in 1966, including a 28-20 victory over Florida State in the Sun Bowl. Eaton welcomed him back in 1969, and the outspoken Hamilton was one of the "Black 14" booted from the nationally-ranked Cowboys squad by the head coach for requesting permission to wear black armbands prior to the Oct. 18 game against Brigham Young University. The players wanted to protest the Mormon Church's policy prohibiting blacks from holding the priesthood. Eaton's rash decision, only a season removed from Wyoming's appearance in the Sugar Bowl, sent the program into a tailspin as the Cowboys – who had a 31-4 record in the 35 games prior to the Black 14 incident – went 20-51 over the next 6 1/2 seasons.

"It kind of scared me at first because I knew everyone of the Black 14 could have played pro. I knew if we stood up it could damage our careers," Ivie Moore, one of the players kicked off the team, recalled. "But I knew at some point in time you've got to stand up for what you believe in. And after thinking about it, I stood up."

Three years earlier, Strannigan's basketball program was finally taking off with a 17-9 finish in 1966, an NCAA Tournament appearance in 1967, back-to-back NIT appearances in 1968 and 1969, and a 19-win campaign in 1970. But Wyoming also struggled on the hardwood after the Black 14 incident, compiling a 55-101 record from the start of the 1970-71 season through the 1974-75 season.

On Dec. 29, 1962, Wyoming lost 93-82 to Loyola-Chicago, which had broken the "gentleman's agreement" among coaches not to play more than three black players at once in 1961 and became the first team in Division I history to use an all-black lineup, doing so against the Cowboys at a tournament in Oklahoma City. Jimerson stayed the course after Bostick's departure and averaged 17.5 points during his senior season in 1962 while doing his best to mentor his physically gifted new roommate, Flynn Robinson.

"We only had a couple of black players. Curt was one of the captains," said Robinson, who averaged a Wyoming-record 26.3 pointer per game from 1963-65 and won an NBA championship with the Los Angeles Lakers in 1972. "I roomed with him and he was a good example for me. A very good example."

After graduating from Wyoming in 1963 with a degree in education, Jimerson returned to El Paso only months before John F. Kennedy's Dallas assassination rocked the country. Bobby Kennedy, the Attorney General, was starting to put pressure on FBI Director J. Edgar Hoover to hire more black agents.

"Hoover was something else. He had blacks with FBI credentials as special agents. But he used them as a chauffeur and a receptionist," Jimerson said. "So if anybody asked if he had black agents, he would say yes. Bobby Kennedy found out what he was doing."

Jimerson's dad mentioned to him that a recruiter had been by his lodge looking for blacks interested in working for the FBI. Although overqualified, Jimerson accepted a clerical position and became the first black employee at the FBI office in El Paso. After gaining some work experience and also serving in Vietnam, Jimerson received his appointment as an FBI agent in 1968, making history once again.

"I was one of the first 12 or 13 black agents legitimately hired," Jimerson said. "I was in a class of 28 in Quantico, Virginia. I was the only black guy and the only one in the class who knew where I was headed. The day after you graduate they hand you an envelope that has the name of the city where you are headed. I already knew I was coming to Oakland, California, to work the Black Panthers."

Before a distinguished FBI career in the, Jimerson was in Fort Bragg, North Carolina, preparing to head to Vietnam when he watched Texas Western soar over a racial hurdle in major college basketball by beating Adolph Rupp's all-white Kentucky team in the NCAA championship game using an all-black starting five. Jimerson had grown up playing with many of the members of Don Haskins' "Glory Road" team in a summer league in El Paso.

"Four starters on that Texas Western team played together on a city league team that played against my Union Furniture team," Jimerson said. "It made me feel so good when they won because in that league I was MVP. I was real happy for them."
Jimerson also grew up competing against Nolan Richardson, who played at Texas Western from 1960-64 and coached Arkansas to the NCAA title in 1994.

"Nolan was at Bowie High, and I was at Austin. We played on a team called the Texas All-Stars that traveled to Mexico and played their Olympic team in 1964," Jimerson said. "It was so cool to see Nolan do what he did."

At Wyoming, Jimerson helped open up a door that great players like Robinson, Fennis Dembo and Brandon Ewing would walk through over the years. Some of these legendary Cowboys expressed their gratitude to Jimerson in 2005 during the the 100th anniversary celebration of the program in Laramie.

"I worked for the NBA for seven years, and anytime a Wyoming player came through here I'd be all over them," said Jimerson, who ran the security for the Golden State Warriors after retiring from the FBI. "Wyoming was good to me because it gave me what I needed. My parents wanted me to have a better life and to get a better education. And I was the first of the 10 children to get a college degree . . . .

"It wasn't a party school that I was a part of. I just remember studying because it was too cold to do anything else."

Jimerson and Bostick were thought to be the first black basketball players at Wyoming for decades, but documentation exists that may suggest otherwise. A brochure in 1931 found in the athletic department archives shows two blacks on the football team. One of them is Taft Harris from Casper, whose name appears on the Natrona County High School's hall-of-fame for winning numerous letters. The photographs in that 1931 publication indicate that a player identified as P. Parkhurst may have been an African-American. There is a photo of Harris in the Feb. 10, 1932, edition of The Branding Iron, next to a photo of Ed McGinty, with the following description of the pair:

Cowboy Reserves who will be raring to get a chance at the Tigers Friday and Saturday. These two men have in numerous instances shown their ability to pinch hit for the regulars and are now waiting to get their chance at Colorado College.

McGinty, Harris and the rest of the Wyoming players swept the two-game home stand with Colorado College at Half Acre Gym as part of a 13-game winning streak. The 1931-32 Cowboys finished with an amazing 18-2 record. There is a photo, which has been published in the program's media guide over the years, of head coach Willard Witte receiving the Rocky Mountain Athletic Conference championship trophy at the end of the season after Wyoming, the East Division champion, won two of three games over West Division champion BYU in Laramie. Both teams are also posing in the image. And there is one black face in the crowd – Taft Harris.

"I'm blown away by that," Jimerson said after being presented with photographic evidence that Harris was likely the first black basketball player at Wyoming 29 years before he stepped foot on campus. "I just can't imagine that."

It is amazing that Taft was competing on the football field and inside Half Acre Gym for the Cowboys in 1931, considering Jackie Robinson – who famously broke the color barrier in Major League Baseball with the Brooklyn Dodgers in 1947 – was 13 years old when Taft was playing varsity sports at Wyoming. Nat Northington and Greg Page, who played at Kentucky beginning in 1966, were the first black football players in the Southeastern Conference. The first black basketball player in the SEC was Maryland's Billy Jones (1965-66). In 1970, a year after the Black 14 incident, BYU recruited its first black football player (Ron Knight). The first black basketball player to lace them up at BYU was Danny Frazier during the 1977-78 season. That's a 46-year gap from Taft's playing days in Laramie.

Wyoming football programs from 1946-60 indicate that no African-Americans played on those teams. Very few appear among the photos of the opposing teams, either. One of them was James Jordan, a halfback on the Denver Pioneers when they played at Memorial Stadium in 1949. The first black football player at Wyoming in the post-World War II era appears to be Mike Walker, a sophomore halfback from Detroit, who appears in the 1961 football game programs. Walker is not there the next year, but Alan Johnson and Dave Marion, both running backs from Bakersfield, California, are shown. In 1963, Earland Ezell, a tailback from Grand Rapids, Michigan, appears in the programs. Beginning in 1964 and most likely continuing each year until the present day, the Cowboys' rosters have included at least two blacks. Besides the three members of the Black 14 who returned to the team in 1970, the roster that year included three new black players and by 1972 that number was up to nine.

Taft died on March 28, 1961, and is buried at Highland Cemetery in Casper, Wyoming. His obituary in the Casper Tribune-Herald – headlined "Taft Harris, Negro Athlete Here, Is Dead" – read as follows:

Taft Harris, well-known former athlete and prominent member of the Negro community in Casper, died Tuesday at St. Luke's Hospital Denver, after a lengthy illness. He was 49.

Born Sept. 7, 1911, in Eldorado, Arkansas, Harris came to Casper at the age of nine to live with his sister, Mrs. Alabama Hart.

He attended Casper schools and was the first four-letter man in three sports, gaining recognition in football, basketball and track. He was also honored with membership in the Football Hall of Fame at Natrona County High School. In his junior and senior years, he was also a member of the high school band.

After graduation from high school, Harris attended the University of Iowa for one year, then transferred to the University of Wyoming where he remained until graduation. He played basketball for the university while a student in Laramie.

Upon his return to Casper, Harris was employed at the courthouse for a number of years and in 1944 went to the West Coast as an employee of North American Aviation Company during the war. He was later employed at the Noble Hotel in Lander and returned to Casper in 1949 to take a job with the Ohio Oil Company He continued in that company's employ until his death.

Harris was a deacon of the Second Baptist Church in Casper and a member of the Zenith Masonic Lodge, number 25, Colorado Jurisdiction.

Harris is survived by a son and daughter-in-law, Mr. and Mrs. Taft Harris Jr., of Casper; a daughter and son-in-law, Mr. and Mrs. Charles Finley Jr., of Los Angeles; his sister, Mrs. Hart; a brother, Arthur Gantt, of San Francisco; and another brother, the Rev. John Harris of Magnolia, Arkansas; his mother, Mrs. Rhoda Wysinger, of Eldorado, Arkansas; and one grandchild.

The Jump Shot is Born

Kenneth L. Sailors was born on Jan. 14, 1921, in Bushnell, Nebraska, a rural town located between Kimball, Nebraska, and Pine Bluffs, Wyoming His mother, Cora Belle, had arrived in the Wild West in a covered wagon when she was just a girl. His father, Edward, was a farmer who decided he wasn't going to be happy raising a large family. Cora Belle delivered baby Kenny in his bedroom. Just the two of them. Both tough as nails.

"It was just my mother and I. No doctors, no midwives, she took care of everything," Sailors said.

Kenny didn't really get a chance to know Edward, who left Cora Belle when Kenny was an infant, and, died in the 1950s. Kenny was the youngest of six children. Three of his sisters were born triplets and died at birth.

"My dad was pretty unhappy with her at the time I was born," Sailors said of Cora Belle. "My mom was in her 40s then."

When Kenny was about 4, Cora Belle moved the family to a 320-acre farm located a few miles south of tiny Hillsdale, Wyoming, a desolate prairie town located approximately 19 miles east of Cheyenne. Kenny's older brother Bud, his best friend and role model, worked hard to help make sure the family survived the Great Depression.

"Mom got along fine. Some summers we'd have 30 to 40 acres of potatoes. Bud was five years older and he would cultivate the potatoes and other crops and he'd get the weeds on both sides. My job and my mom's job were to get the weeds in the middle," Sailors recalled. "Bud got to be old for an 8- or 9-year-old kid. One day I said, 'I'm tired of getting potatoes.' She told me to, 'Go ahead and get my hoe and go to the house. Just don't come to the dinner table tonight . . . .'

"She was a good mother. She taught my brother and me both a lot of the real important things in life. They say a woman can't raise boys without a husband. That's a bunch of nonsense."

Although Bud had become the man of the house, Cora Belle clearly wore the pants in the family.

"I remember one time Bud, he must have said 'Damn!' or 'Hell!' And momma pulled him into kitchen by the hair and washed his mouth out with lye soap," Sailors said with a wry grin. "He lived to be 89, and I never heard him swear again."

No matter what harsh Wyoming weather they faced, the Sailors would faithfully ride horses from the farm on Sunday mornings to a little white church four miles down the road in Hillsdale.

"Mom read the Bible to us in the evening and talked about different passages," Sailors said. "That had an affect on my life."

The small 40-student school the boys attended, called the Hillsdale Consolidated District, had a basketball program, which provided a great escape for Bud and Kenny. The grade school kids even played games against teams from other nearby Wyoming towns like Albin, Burns, and Carpenter. Bud, who spouted to 6-foot-5, naturally developed into a standout varsity player for Hillsdale coach Floyd Domine, who even let his star center take a ball home to work on his game. Little did Domine know that the gesture would help change the history of the sport.

Over 75 years later, sitting in his one-bedroom apartment in Laramie, Wyoming, just steps away from majestic War Memorial Stadium on the University of Wyoming campus, Kenny recalls the spring afternoon in 1934 when he revolutionized the game of basketball as clearly as if the madness took place last March. Kenny and Bud were shooting a worn-out old leather ball at a rusted iron hoop and crude backboard, which they had carefully measured to 10 feet and attached to a windmill on the family farm. The playing surface was dirt. The rim was naked, no net. The shoes were hand-me-downs, nothing like the Nikes kids require from their parents today. And the most difficult challenge for Kenny was simply getting a shot off over Bud's elongated, seemingly boundless outstretched arms.

"We would get to play some on weekends and in the summertime. We worked hard during the Depression in order to stay alive. There wasn't any money," Kenny said. "I remember I was in the eighth grade, and Bud used to laugh at me and have fun slapping that ball down on me. I really couldn't get a shot off on him. He was 6-5, which was a big man in those days, and a good ball player."

Kenny eventually topped out at 5-10. He weighed 138 pounds soaking wet. That didn't stop him from eventually becoming a relentless defensive end on the football field, as well as a state track and field champion in the mile and broad jump. Kenny's size, or lack thereof, didn't cause him to shy away from the challenge of competing one-on-one against Bud in basketball, either. As a result of his determination to beat Bud, the scrawnier Sailors, 13 at the time, invented a move Jerry West, Michael Jordan, and LeBron James would take for granted decades later.

"The one thing I could do was jump. I could broad jump and high jump when I was just a punk kid. I had legs on me and I could get up. I won state here in Laramie with a broad jump of 22 feet as a senior," Kenny explained. So I thought, "That guy is big, and I'm not very big. But I can jump."

"So I decided to run right at Bud and jump straight up. I leaped as high as I could and shot the ball over him. I don't remember if it was one-handed or two-handed, but I made one."

And so the jump shot was invented — or at the very least perfected — by Sailors, literally on Wyoming soil.

Bud, a skilled center, had led Hillsdale to a district title and an appearance in the state tournament a few years earlier. In those days, the ball came back to mid-court for a jump after every made basket. So Bud dominated the game from start to finish with his size. One evening the lanky local star scored 39 points against Burns, outscoring the opposition by himself. The dedicated Sailors brothers usually arrived at school 45 minutes early, and Domine would leave a basketball, the old model that zipped up, out in the gym so they could get some shots up.

"I thought my big brother was something else," Kenny said. "He had quite an influence on me."

Kenny was reluctant to show off his revolutionary stroke as a kid. Domine, like almost every coach in the country, taught his players to only leave the floor to grab rebounds.

"I didn't dare to do the jump shot much around coaches because they would shoot you down. You weren't allowed to leave your feet on offense or defense," Kenny said.

Meanwhile, Bud nearly helped write a Hoosiers story for Hillsdale, leading the high school team to the 1935 state tournament in Casper. Bud and his six teammates lost in the semifinals to eventual state champion Rock Springs.

"Back then only 16 teams went to the state tournament. Wheatland was the biggest school in our district, and Hillsdale ended up playing Wheatland at home to see who got to go to state," Kenny said. "We couldn't house all of them who wanted to watch that game in the gym. We ended up beating them, even though there weren't 30 people in the town."

In 1936, Cora Belle sold the farm, and the Sailors moved to Laramie, where Bud had enrolled at the University of Wyoming. Bud, a big man on the small campus, played some basketball for the Cowboys under head coach Dutch Witte, while moonlighting as a taxi driver to help pay for his education. Kenny was quickly emerging as a local basketball star at Laramie High School. When Kenny was a sophomore, he went to a national AAU Tournament in Denver and saw Hank Luisetti play. While earning All-American honors at Stanford in the 1930s, Luisetti developed an unstoppable one-handed shot while everyone else was still relying on the two-handed set shot.

"(Luisetti) had a step-and-shoot move," Sailors said. "I think that's where I copied the one-handed shot from him."

Luisetti didn't leave the floor with both feet before releasing his shot. It was Sailors who would take the idea of the jump shot to new heights.

"Luisetti and Kenny Sailors of Wyoming have to be the two who most influenced the game in my time," legendary St. John's player and head coach Joe Lapchick told the New York Sunday News after retiring in 1965, 22 years after his NIT champion team lost to NCAA champion Wyoming in a charity game at Madison Square Garden. "Sailors started the one-handed jumper, which is probably the shot of the present and future."

To a rural farm kid, the college town of Laramie felt like a metropolis. Kenny tried to talk Cora Belle into letting him trade his bib overalls in for waist pants so his peers would quit snickering at him in the cruel high school hallways. She said no, but Kenny made it clear to the other students that they couldn't pick on the new kid without a fight. Eventually, Bud helped his brother out by giving him a pair of Levis.

Sports continued to be a great escape for Kenny. The basketball coach at Laramie High School in the late 1930s was Floyd Foreman, who also coached football and track. His star transfer from Hillsdale continued to master the jump shot, and some equally mesmerizing dribbling skills, on a basket Bud had hung on the garage at the Sailors residence at 168 North 5th.

"(Foreman) was a real good coach in my opinion. He never tried to stop me," Sailors said. "And I didn't shoot the jump shot a lot in high school. I got to where I could dribble into the center around the free throw line and get a shot off just about any time I wanted to. I was still experimenting."

Kenny, an all-state selection, led the Plainsmen to back-to-back runner-up finishes at the state tournament as a junior in 1938 and senior in 1939. Rock Springs, led by future Wyoming All-American and head coach Bill Strannigan, hung the championship banners at the expense of another Sailors. Believe it or not, Cora Belle's feisty son actually enjoyed the gridiron more than the hardwood as a prep standout. Kenny was a two-time all-state pick in football.

"In high school, I liked football better than basketball," Sailors said. "I really loved football."

After graduation, Kenny enrolled at Wyoming with dreams of being a three-sport star for the Cowboys like Milward Simpson (the only student-athlete to captain the University's baseball, basketball and football teams during his playing days from 1917-21). Ev Shelton, the impressive first-year head coach of the Cowboy basketball program, had a different plan for Kenny.

"Shelton said, 'Sailors, I hear you're going out for football? If you're going to fool around, don't play basketball,'" Sailors said.

The cocky freshman told Foreman about Shelton's ultimatum.

"Coach Foreman kind of smiled at me and said, 'Kenny, you've got to remember you only weigh about 140 pounds. It's a pretty tough go to play football, especially at left end,'" Sailors said. "I tried to wrestle too, and they wouldn't let me do that, either. Everett Lance was a good friend of mine and he wanted me to come out. We didn't have wrestling in high school, but I was doing pretty well in intramurals. Of course, Shelton thought I'd be so muscle bound that I wouldn't be able to shoot a basketball."

Soon Shelton and Sailors would be on the same page and on the way to making history together.

In late March 1986, Jim Brandenburg recaptured the imagination of the Wyoming fan base and put a talented young group of Cowboys in the East Coast spotlight by guiding the program to the NIT championship game at Madison Square Garden. The Pokes, led by super sophomores Fennis Dembo and Eric Leckner, beat Texas A&M, Loyola-Marymount, Clemson and

Florida during the tournament before losing to Ohio State in the title game.

"I did not realize the reverence that the New York basketball fans had for the University of Wyoming, until I took the '86 team to the NIT," Brandenburg said. "I cannot tell you how well we were received in New York. The old newspaper guys reminded me about all of the Wyoming teams that had played at Madison Square Garden all the way back to the NCAA championship team. That '43 team not only won the NCAA championship, they stayed and beat the NIT champs. Back in those days all the real media coverage was on the East Coast, and they thought the NIT champions were the best, until upstart Wyoming goes in there and beats their ass, too."

Sailors and the Cowboys had already beaten CCNY at the Garden on Dec, 30, 1941, during a 15-5 season. In 1942-43, Shelton's program forever etched itself in college basketball lore with a victory over Georgetown on the same floor for the NCAA title, followed by a 52-47 overtime triumph over NIT champion St. John's for undisputed national bragging rights. After returning from World War II, Sailors was photographed by Life Magazine taking his gravity-defying jump shot during a 57-42 victory over Long Island at the Garden on Jan. 3, 1946.

"I heard of Kenny Sailors," recalled Brandenburg, who was a schoolboy in San Antonio, Texas, when the Cowboys were making national headlines in the 1940s. "Most of the high school coaches in Texas were still teaching the underhanded free throw or the two-handed push shot. We were just starting to develop the one-handed set shot, more the one-handed step shot and the step-back one-hander. We knew about the jump shot, but we didn't have any coaches that could really teach us step by step, so we could really get into it. We knew that Kenny was one of the guys credited for starting the jump shot . . . .

"Of course, the jump shot just revolutionized the game. But it wasn't like Kenny went to New York and everybody starting shooting the jump shot. It took a while for coaches to get used to it. Coaches did not have a progressive set of skill sets they would teach. Kids would develop their own style of shooting, and coaches would set team offense and team defense. Once the cat was out of the bag and the jump shot was introduced, it has become such a predominant part of the game. Kenny was a tremendous athlete, and I truly think he is the guy who should be fully credited for the innovation of the jump shot."

Curt Gowdy, who played with Sailors at Wyoming before becoming an American broadcasting icon, once said that Jumpin' Johnny Adams was the original jump shooter. The Arkansas All-American led the Razorbacks to a 52-40 victory over Wyoming in the 1941 NCAA Tournament.

"That shot changed the game of basketball," Gowdy recalled in the well-researched book The Origins of the Jump Shot. "Who was the first jump shooter? Coaches, broadcasters – every year at the Final Four, we stand around and argue about it. I say it was Johnny Adams." An account of the game in the "Laramie Daily Bulletin" described Adams' performance this way:

A kinky-haired, spindle-legged lad named John Adams employed a freakish two-handed jump shot that went straight for the basket and dropped through on 11 occasions from the field and four more times at the free throw line for a total of 26 points, to do the major portion in counting out the Cowboy quintet.

Shelton countered with his own jump-shooting star, bringing Sailors off the bench a little too late.

Meanwhile, little Kenneth Sailors was doing the biggest part of the futile job of whittling down the towering Razorbacks, who are thus far undefeated this season in 19 collegiate games. Forced to shoot far out after beautiful maneuvering, Sailors whipped six goals and five free throws through to account for 17 points.

Arkansas jumped into a lead on the opening tip off and was never headed. After the first seven minutes of play the Razorbacks led, 13-4, and held a similar margin of 29-18 at the half.

When the second period opened, Coach Shelton had his five covering all over the court, and by dint of real hustle and inspired drive, managed to keep within close range of the eventual winners throughout the final half.

Sailors counted three times in quick succession and Curtis Gowdy and Bill Strannigan followed suit to pull the losers up to within 31-35 distance. At this point, Adams contracted Sailors' scoring tactics and hit three baskets in rapid fire succession to clinch the game for the tree top-tall team.

The Naismith Memorial Basketball Hall of Fame suggests that yet another player, Glenn Roberts, may have been the first to shoot a jumper. Roberts, a Virginian, used a two-handed jump shot in the early- and mid-1930s while in high school and at Emory & Henry College. Joe Fulks is also considered to be one of the "fathers" of this shot, honing his skills with it as a kid in

Kentucky before attending Murray State and then playing from 1946-1962 with the NBA's Philadelphia Warriors. In a New York Times article, John Miller Cooper, who played at Missouri, described his shot in a 1931 game this way: "My feet left the hardcourt surface, and it felt good. It was free and natural, and I knew I had discovered something." Interestingly, Cooper's first shots were taken at a barrel hoop nailed to the side of a cattle farm smokehouse. Another jump-shooting pioneer, North Carolina's Belus Van Smawley, honed his skills using a peach basket hung at a railroad depot. The Origins of the Jump Shot author, John Christgau, also included Moose Gonzales, Minnesota All-American Myer "Whitey" Skoog, San Francisco State's John "Mouse" Gonzales, and Princeton's Bud Palmer in his list of "Eight Men Who Shook the World of Basketball."

Many credible basketball historians and legendary coaches from the era consider Sailors to be the first pure jump shooter. Ray Meyer, a Naismith Hall of Fame member who coached DePaul to 13 NCAA Tournaments and eight NIT appearances, piling up a 724-354 record from 1942-84, sent Sailors the following letter:

Dear Kenny,

I remember you well from your playing days at Wyoming. You beat us at the Chicago Stadium. Then you went on to play five ball for a few years.

The first man I ever saw shoot the one-handed shot was Blair Varnes who played for De Paul University in the late 20's. The next was Roscoe from Minnesota. He was a football player who had a shoulder dislocated. His left arm was strapped so he couldn't raise it above his shoulder. Neither one of these men shot a one handed jump shot. It was a stand still shot.

Hank Luisetti of Stanford played '36, '37, & '38. He played when I did. I never saw him play, but I always believed it was a set one handed.

Kenny, You were the first one I saw who really had a one-handed jump shot. There were variations, but I never saw one who actually used the true one handed shot.

Joe Fulk's shot was not a one handed jump shot. He could shoot – I saw him play many times.

Kenny, I don't speak or write as an authority, but you were the first I saw with the true jump shot as we know it today.

Good luck to you, Kenny!

Yours,

Ray Meyer

Due to Sailors' influence, many of the 1943 Cowboys adopted their own versions of the modern jump shot, which made Wyoming one of the most exciting and influential teams to ever participate in the NCAA Tournament.

"We were the only team around in those days where everybody shot one-handed," guard Floyd Volker told the Hartford Courant 50 years after Wyoming's NCAA title. "You know, the Easterners all clicked their heels and shot two-handed. But we shot everything with one hand, even our free-throws. They loved our style at Madison Square Garden. We were voted the most popular team to play there that year."

On Jan. 14, 2011, the Wyoming basketball program celebrated Kenny's 90th birthday during the Cowboys' game against Utah at the Arena-Auditorium, where the living legend's number 4 jersey and the 1943 NCAA championship banner proudly hang from the rafters of the program's modern home. The modest old basketball trailblazer appreciates all the attention, but Sailors notes: "Who could really say who invented the jump shot? Somebody else probably jumped in the air somewhere and shot a ball before me."

Kenny Sailors' story, however, is the one that sticks. And he thanks to Cora Belle's tough, unconditional love during his childhood, Bud's towering presence in front of the windmill basket, and Shelton's visionary coaching for that.

"I'm pretty proud of the fact that people think highly of me," Sailors said. "Frankly, I've never thought that highly of myself. There have been plenty of other good ballplayers at Wyoming."

The Mythical Cowboy

Wyoming has produced some accomplished NBA players through the decades. Theo Ratliff just wrapped up a 15-year career that included an appearance in the 2001 All-Star Game and leading the league in blocked shots three times. Flynn Robinson also made an All-Star Game appearance, led the league in free throw percentage and was a key member of the Los Angeles Lakers' dominant championship team in 1972. Bill Garnett was the number 4 overall pick in the 1982 draft. Chris Engler, Eric Leckner and Reggie Slater had solid careers as journeymen. Fennis Dembo (Detroit Pistons) and Tim Breaux (Houston Rockets) have NBA championship rings. Fittingly, Kenny Sailors was the first big-name Cowboy to enjoy more than a cup of coffee in professional basketball.

"Nothing like college ball," is how Sailors remembers his five-year run in the fledgling NBA from 1946-51. "Back then you were playing for money, but you had to end up in the top 10 in scoring if you wanted to keep your salary. And I did. I was up there every year in assists and scoring."

Sailors turned 26 during his first season in the Basketball Association of America (BAA), a league that laid the foundation for the modern-day National Basketball Association (NBA), which was founded in 1949. The well-known Wyoming star played for the Cleveland Rebels during the BAA's inaugural season in 1946-47. Even at the professional level, the jump shot Sailors created on the farm in Hillsdale, perfected at Half Acre Gym in Laramie, and made famous at Madison Square Garden in New York, was not universally embraced. Sailors only averaged 9.9 points and 2.3 assists as a rookie. Cleveland coach Red "Dutch" Dehnert was not a fan of the game's evolution and kept the three-time All-American on the bench in favor of stiff, set-shooting starters.

"Dutch said, 'Sailors, if you're going to make it in this league you're going to have to learn the two-handed set shot,'" Sailors recalled.

Fortunately for Sailors and professional basketball, Dehnert was sent out on the road as a scout and replaced as coach in the middle of the season. The Wyoming kid was finally put on the floor and allowed to play with his revolutionary style, and as a result, the Rebels rallied from a slow start to make the playoffs. Getting the BBA off the ground, at a time when baseball was the true national pastime, and college basketball was much more popular than professional hoops, proved to be a tough road for players and franchises during the era. The Rebels folded after one season, and Sailors' rights were awarded to the Chicago Stags via a random drawing.

"People don't understand it today because they don't even come close to doing it that way anymore. But in my day, in the early NBA, a lot of teams were getting in for a year and getting out. They operated on shoe-string budgets," Sailors explained. "Cleveland, the team I played for the first year I was in the NBA, played just one year and got out . . . . The way they handled that was when a franchise dropped out of the league, they no longer owned the players. And the players then became property of the league. Of course, the league didn't want them. (Maurice) Podoloff was the name of the (BAA) commissioner in those days and all during my years in the NBA. We were property of the league to start with, and then the commissioner very shortly after that would call a meeting in New York with all the owners. They would literally draw out of a hat. If they drew one of us (from a defunct franchise) and used us, we became a part of their ball team. Then they had to get rid of one of their men, either sell him, trade him, or release him. You could only have 12 players."

"The year Cleveland dropped out of the league it was the Chicago Stags that drew my name out of the hat. Well, I wasn't there very long. They try to get rid of you just as soon as they can because they don't want you around if they don't want to keep you. They'll hold you long enough to sell you or trade you and get something out of the deal. I ended up in a three-way deal, I don't know if there was cash involved or how it worked, but I ended up in a three-way deal between the Stags to Philadelphia for not much more than a week and finally ended up in Providence."

After playing one game for Chicago and two for Philadelphia at the start of the 1947-48 season, Sailors proved to be a good fit in Providence with the Steamrollers, averaging 12.7 points. George Duffy, the Steamrollers' publicist, wrote the following news release in 1947 to help get New England basketball fans excited about the team's new star:

> His jump-shot was "out of this world" as one veteran newspaper man remarked. The kids of the state began to copy the shot. In Boys' clubs, YMCAs, Church leagues, and every other youthful circuit around the state, the kids jumped and shot and always remarked, "That's the way Kenny Sailors does it!"

Yes, the "Wyoming Kid" had won his way into the hearts of every basketball fan, his cat-like defensive play, his swift dribbling, and the jump-shot all added up to real basketball entertainment.

During the 1948-49 season, Sailors averaged 15.8 points and 3.7 assists per game to lead Providence. Howie Shannon (13.4) and Chuck Halbert (11.4) were also scoring in double figures, and Sailors' backcourt running mate, Ernie Calverley, was adding 9.4 points and 4.3 assists. But the Steamrollers were still getting steamrolled for the most part, averaging 78.5 points and yielding 87.1 points per game en route to a 12-48 record.

"I kind of liked it in Providence, although I hated going back to that East Coast. Too many people, and I couldn't take my wife because she had asthma," Sailors said. "I liked the owner, Lou Pieri, and what I didn't realize at that time is Lou and Walter Brown of the Boston Celtics were actually working together."

Indeed, Pieri and Brown, the president of the Celtics, had agreed to merge the two franchises due to the saturation of the market, given the close proximity of Providence and Boston. Neither team enjoyed much success in three BAA seasons with the Celtics compiling a 67-101 record and the Steamrollers struggling with a 46-122 mark. History shows the correct decision was made to fold the Providence franchise and make Boston one of the original NBA teams in 1949. Sailors, frustrated with the instability of the Providence franchise and a little homesick, headed back to the Rocky Mountains and played for the original Denver Nuggets during the inaugural NBA season. He averaged a career-high 17.3 points and 4.0 assists in 57 games during the 1949-50 season. Denver proved to be the dregs of the new league, however, finishing with a dismal 11-51 record. Sailors' Nuggets trading card listed the 28-year-old at 5-11 and 160 pounds with the following description of his skills:

Anyone who reads the sports pages is familiar with the exploits of fabulous Kenny Sailors, as great a player as was ever produced by the basketball crazed University of Wyoming. Sailors' name has frequently been linked with the most well-known aspirants of cagedom, and he has certainly earned his way.

He is one of the fastest men in basketball today, and probably the game's best dribbler. Sailors usually turns up on the court when and where he is least expected, and besides being a deadly accurate jump shot artist, he is practically unguardable. He has behind him a colorful career at the University of Wyoming, in addition to having compiled enviable professional records while a member of the Cleveland Rebels, Chicago Stags and Providence Steamrollers.

Best known for pioneering the jump shot, Sailors had impressive dribbling skills that were also something to behold. At Wyoming, coach Ev Shelton never had to worry about breaking a full-court press with Sailors on the floor.

"No team could press us because of (Sailors') ball-handling abilities," Floyd Volker said. "No one or two men could get the ball from him, he was that good. We would spread out and just turn him loose and listen to the crowd applaud."

Sailors developed the jump shot at 13 out on the farm using the old hoop attached to the windmill. He learned to dribble out of trouble at an even earlier age at the school in Hillsdale, where coach Floyd Domine would leave a ball in the gym for the students to fight over every morning.

"I learned to dribble when I was 6 or 7, going to grade school in Hillsdale. We'd ride the bus in from the farm and we'd get into the school early, and the old coach would leave an old basketball out. All of us kids in that age group, we'd all make a rush for the gym to get the ball," Sailors said. "The first one that got it, you could start dribbling anywhere in the gym, but the minute you stopped and picked the ball up they could grab you or tackle you or anything else to get the ball. So you had to keep dribbling around the whole gym, and they'd try and take it away from you. It got pretty rough sometimes, but we did that every morning for three or four years."

Ironically, following a productive year in Denver, Sailors ended up playing with Bob Cousy – perhaps the most famous ball handler in NBA history – during the infancy of the emerging Celtics' dynasty. The Nuggets were also one-and-done, going out of business after Sailors' high-scoring season in the Mile High City, and the Celtics grabbed Sailors' rights out of the hat in New York. The problem was that Sailors didn't get along very well with the brash, young, cigar-smoking coach by the name of Red Auerbach.

"Well, I certainly didn't want to play for Auerbach. He had known me when I was in the Marine Corps. He didn't particularly want me to be playing for him, and I didn't particularly want to play for him," Sailors said. "He did a great job bringing in some great players. But his greatest ability wasn't as a coach, it was bringing in some of the greatest ball players the NBA has ever had. They won championships for him."

Auerbach was not initially a fan of the Celtics' popular rookie point guard either, however, Cousy quickly won him over with his dazzling play on the court, leading Boston to six NBA titles while appearing in 13 All-Star Games and being named the league's most valuable player in 1957.

"Auerbach came out and said Cousy was a great college ball player, but he'd never go in the pros because he had too much of this behind-the-back type of dribbling and stuff," Sailors said. "I admire Cousy for it, he never took after Red. Chuck Cooper and I helped Cousy deal with that."

Meanwhile, Auerbach kept Sailors on the bench throughout his 60-game stay in Boston. Imagine the possibilities if Cousy was setting up Sailors for open jump shots? Eight years after leading Wyoming to the national championship, Sailors' basketball career came to an end with the Baltimore Bullets. He teamed up with another early jump shooter, Belus Smawley, and averaged 8.2 points and 2.5 assists a game on another substandard team (the Bullets finished 24-42 that season). Not surprisingly, the NBA isn't Sailors' favorite subject.

"The pros didn't appeal to me that much," Sailors said. "I played long enough to get my pension. Then I came home to be with my family."

Sailors made $7,500 during his most memorable season in Providence, which was an impressive salary in the years after World War II. Nike and Gatorade didn't exist, but the jump-shooting star did land endorsement deals pitching bubble gum and prune juice. As Sailors traveled from team to team and city to city – often by car or bus – during his professional playing career, his better half, Marilynne, was back home in Wyoming putting the paychecks in the bank.

"My wife and my mother were the two most influential people in my life for sure," Sailors said. "We were married 60 years, so we had a pretty good life together. Wonderful woman."

The competitive Sailors dabbled in politics after stepping away from the basketball spotlight. He was a representative for Laramie County in the Wyoming Legislature in 1955-56. He ran for Wyoming's seat in the U.S. House of Representatives but lost to William Henry Harrison in the primary. In 1964, he ran for U.S. Senate and lost again.

"I'm glad I didn't win because it would have killed my wife," Sailors said. "Her condition with her asthma and emphysema, she couldn't have done well in Washington D.C. She lived to be 79. The doctors told me when she was 20 that she'd probably be fortunate to make it until she was 50. We didn't tell her that, but they told me that. They didn't have ways of helping people with asthma and emphysema in those days like they do today."

Kenny and Marilynne, due to concerns with her health but also because of their love of the untamed West and spirit of adventure, spent the next four decades as dude ranchers and hunting and fishing guides. The couple used the NBA money to buy the Heart Six Ranch in Jackson, Wyoming, and later moved to an even more remote and pristine spread in Gakona, Alaska.

"I didn't even know we had that money. She was saving those checks the whole time I was gone. We bought the Heart Six Ranch and really enjoyed it. Our kids grew up there and they both graduated from Jackson High School. They loved it. They loved the horses and the outdoors," Sailors said. "We handled dudes and we weren't too happy with that operation. Spoiled kids were beginning to control everything and their parents didn't do anything about it. So we decided to go to Alaska. For that business, guiding and outfitting, there was nothing like it when we went up there to the Wrangell Mountains and the Gulkana River . . . the king salmon, the red salmon, the rainbow trout, the caribou herds, the moose, the brown bears, the white sheep . . . ."

"I sure miss going up there. I'm getting a little too old to go out on these rivers alone and walk around on these slippery rocks. You get to be 90, you have to give a little of that up."

Sailors did not give the game of basketball up in Alaska. He lobbied for the local schools to start girls basketball programs and coached the Glenallen girls to a state championship while teaching history at the tiny school. Later, the Sailors lived on Admiralty Island, in Angoon, a village of the Tinglit tribe, where he was also a successful high school coach.

There is no excuse for why Sailors – a three-time All-American, a national champion, a jump shot pioneer, and a successful NBA player – is not a member of the Naismith Memorial Hall of Fame in Springfield, Massachusetts, or the National Collegiate Basketball Hall of Fame in Kansas City, Missouri The explanation most experts come up with is the fact that he went off the grid for so many years living a simple life with Marilynne and his family.

"We didn't have newspapers or radio or anything," Sailors said. "We couldn't follow Wyoming. I guess they all kind of lost track of me. They ask me why I'm not in the hall of fame, and probably the biggest reason is I just disappeared from society for 35 years. They didn't know where I was and never heard from me."

In 2003, Marilynne died and Kenny decided to return to Laramie, where he enjoys rock star status at every Cowboys and Cowgirls home game.

"He's such a Wyoming treasure. I always call him that, and he doesn't like that. But he is a Wyoming treasure," said Kevin McKinney, the longtime sports information director at Wyoming and color man on the football and basketball radio broadcasts. "Kenny is a sensational human being in terms of his competitiveness. Even today, he comes in often and actually diagrams plays he thinks we should be running. He thinks he can help the Cowgirls every bit as much as he can help the Cowboys. I love to have him come by . . . ."

"It's like having Abe Lincoln in your department after the Civil War and you can talk to him about things that are just mythical to me."

Reggie Slater boxes out a BYU player at the "Dome of Doom."

Theo Ratliff blocks the shot of a New Mexico player.

The great Kenny Sailors, jump shot pioneer and Wyoming's only three-time All-American.

Tony Windis was one of the greatest scorers in Cowboys' history.

Fennis Dembo is interviewed by legendary broadcaster Brent Musburger.

Cowboys standout Mike Jackson goes in for a dunk in front of a packed house at War Memorial Fieldhouse as a Hawaii defender looks on helplessly.

Larry Shyatt, Wyoming's coach during the 1997–98 season, returned to the High Plains in 2011 looking to restore the tradition and glory to the Cowboys program.

Josh Davis celebrates Wyoming's outright Mountain West championship after the Cowboys' clinching victory over Utah on March 2, 2002, at the AA.

Kenny Sailors in action at Madison Square Garden during NCAA champion Wyoming's historic 52-47 overtime victory over NIT champion St. John's on April 1, 1943. Cowboys All-American center Milo Komenich (17) looks on.

Eric Leckner, one of the greatest post players in WAC history, puts in a layup against Air Force at the Arena-Auditorium in Laramie.

Built for the Final Four

Jim Brandenburg was born in Topeka, Kansas, on Dec. 10, 1935. At the time, Dr. Forrest C. "Phog" Allen was still the coach at Kansas in nearby Lawrence. When Allen played for the Jayhawks, his coach was Dr. James Naismith. But Brandenburg branched out before becoming a masterful basketball coach in his own right. His family moved to San Antonio, Texas, where he played football in the fall, basketball in the winter, ran track in the spring, and played American Legion baseball in the summer.

"My junior and senior year we made the playoffs in football. My senior year in basketball we lost in the state championship," said Brandenburg, who attended Thomas Edison High School from 1949-53. "Considering the number of schools that participated, if you can get to the state finals, That's a pretty good run. I played on a team that lost a state championship, and from there I went to CSU."

As in Colorado State University. Yes, Brandenburg – one of the icons of Wyoming basketball – played for the rival Rams. Even more interesting, during his freshman season in Fort Collins, the head coach at CSU was Bill Strannigan, the former Cowboys All-American who later became Wyoming's head coach for 14 seasons (1960-73). After Brandenburg's freshman campaign, Strannigan left CSU for Iowa State, where he enjoyed a successful stint in Ames prior to his return to Laramie. Jim Williams became CSU's head coach and not only inherited Brandenburg as a player, but also Boyd "Tiny" Grant, the program's future head coach during the Western Athletic Conference glory days.

"I had a very under-whelming career," Brandenburg said of his college playing days. "I sat the bench and so forth. We had a fantastic coach in Jim Williams. He was one of the best situational basketball coaches I've ever been around. He would create his own offenses where bigs would screen for smalls, and vice versa. He figured out how to get the best player the ball against somebody that couldn't handle them."

During that era, Wyoming's head coach was the legendary Ev Shelton. Brandenburg wisely paid attention not only to Williams' words of wisdom, but also to what the Cowboys coach with the national championship ring was doing on the other bench.

"Usually, we were on the short end of it with Wyoming, but we did have some upset wins," Brandenburg recalled. "What it really was, I had a chance to observe Ev Shelton, a Naismith Hall of Famer and a guy who had won a national championship, and he had very good teams when I was around. Being a player participating, and already thinking I was going to be a coach, I was very observant of Jim Williams, and very aware of what Ev was doing."

After graduating from CSU, Brandenburg returned to San Antonio as a high school coach and later started the Aurora-Hinkley program in metro Denver. He coached one season at Flathead Valley Community College in Kalispell, Montana, building a program from scratch and finishing 24-3 in the inaugural season, before moving on to Montana as an assistant under Jud Heathcote. Brandenburg used his Denver ties to lure a big-time recruit by the name of Michael Ray Richardson to Big Sky country. In his later years at Wyoming, the Cowboys cashed in on a number of overlooked Colorado prospects – Bill Garnett, Mike Jackson, Jon Sommers, and the list goes on – who played like blue-chip recruits in Laramie. During the 1974-75 season, Heathcote and Brandenburg guided Montana to a 21-8 record, the program's first Big Sky championship, and all the way to the NCAA West Regional final, where the Grizzlies lost to UCLA in heartbreaking fashion. The Bruins went on to capture John Wooden's 10th and final NCAA championship.

"The game was in Portland and we actually had them down three with a minute and 20 seconds left. And then we got a bad call," Brandenburg said. "We thought by the middle of the second half we had a chance to beat that team."

After the 1975-76 campaign, Heathcote left for Michigan State, where he would win an NCAA title three years later with Magic Johnson in the most famous championship game of all time (the Spartans beat Larry Bird's Indiana State team in 1979). Brandenburg was promoted to head coach at Montana and hired Mike Montgomery as his assistant. When Brandenburg left for Wyoming, Montgomery became the head coach and hired Stew Morrill as his assistant. When Montgomery left for Stanford, Morrill became head coach and hired Blaine Taylor. Meanwhile, Heathcote's top assistants at Michigan State over the years included Tom Izzo, Tom Crean, Kelvin Sampson and Stan Heath. That's a pretty impressive coaching tree. And Brandenburg is one of the largest branches.

"By the time I was an assistant to Jud I had been in high school coaching for 11 years and had gone to every clinic, bought every book, observed every type of offense or defense, and talked to coaches, picking their brains," Brandenburg said. "When I went with Jud, I had a tremendous amount of knowledge, and what he was able to do was give me a very simple solution to basketball. He taught me to focus all my knowledge into very important parts of the game. Most of what basketball coaches teach is trivial. Really, you just have to concentrate on a few things . . . ."

"Jud has very high IQ. The only other coach I knew with intellect at that level is Bobby Knight."

Sometimes you have to make your own luck. That's what Brandenburg did in 1978 when he dialed the athletic department in Laramie to inquire about becoming the next head coach at Wyoming. The athletic director at the time was George McCartney, who also had the good fortune of hiring Don Haskins at Texas Western (UTEP). That decision led to the Miners making history, becoming the first all-black starting lineup to win a national championship in 1966 at the expense of Adolph Rupp's Kentucky Wildcats. After getting turned down by a couple of other candidates, McCartney wisely picked up the phone and listened to Brandenburg's pitch about how he would get the struggling Cowboys back on the national map.

"With Ev Shelton in the Naismith Hall of Fame and the great football teams and great basketball teams Wyoming had in the past, I had always thought that would be a storied program to coach at," Brandenburg said. "I thought I'd have a chance to get this job. So I called down there."

Life on the high plains wasn't as easy as Brandenburg had imagined. Wyoming had compiled an 84-126 record over the previous eight seasons with just one winning season. Strannigan, after being named WAC Coach of the Year while guiding the Cowboys to an NCAA Tournament appearance and back-to-back NIT appearances, suffered three consecutive losing campaigns to end his tenure. George "Moe" Radovich, another great ex-Wyoming player and a former Strannigan assistant, only lasted three seasons, finishing with a 24-55 record from 1973-76. The program had not been invited to the NCAA Tournament since 1967 and had not enjoyed a 20-win season since 1952-53. The athletic department didn't even sell season tickets for basketball at that time. The band and cheerleaders disbanded after football season. War Memorial Fieldhouse was half-empty for games, and the students that did show up got on the Cowboys as much as the opponents or officials.

"And there was not much talent there, with the exception of two freshmen who were both committed to leave the program," Brandenburg said.

Don DeVoe only coached at Wyoming for two seasons, finishing with a record of 29-25 before leaving abruptly to take the job at Tennessee. However, he deserves credit for recruiting two great Cowboys: Charles Bradley and Kenneth Ollie. Brandenburg's first order of business was to convince the dynamic duo to stay in Laramie.

"My biggest job when I took it was to go back to Birmingham, Alabama, and visit with the Ollie family and Kenneth's high school coach and re-recruit him," Brandenburg said. "And then go back to Maryland and visit with Bradley's mom and family and high school coach. I made the effort and went back to see the parents, and then I just kept working on them and staying on campus more than flitting around trying to find other players . . . ."

"One night I went up into the dorms, Charles and Kenneth were roommates, and I'm talking to them and telling them I wanted them to stay. I guaranteed them a conference championship before their senior year, and they were elbowing each other and snickering. But I believed with those two guys anchoring this basketball program we could do it."

Bradley and Ollie decided to give Brandenburg a chance. The new head coach also retained assistant Tom Asbury, a former standout player at Wyoming, from the previous staff.

"Asbury went to George Washington in Denver and was a good high school player and one of Wyoming's all-time greats," Brandenburg said of the future Kansas State and Pepperdine head coach. "I took the job fairly late, and we weren't close to getting anybody signed. One day I told the secretary to fill out the letter of intent and a scholarship for a player. Tom said, 'What is this?' I told him before the end of the day I would have a player signed."

Brandenburg drove down to Denver and signed Bill Garnett from Regis High School.

"The coach at Regis was Guy Gibbs and he was a great high school coach and he officiated football in the old WAC in the fall. Just a good guy and a good friend," Brandenburg said. "He told me about Bill when I was at Montana. When I left, and this tells you how antiquated things were back then, I told Montgomery,

'Mike, I won't touch Bill Garnett if you want to recruit him.' Mike didn't have any idea of what the potential was for Bill because he had a sprained ankle his senior year. So he was pretty luke-warm about Bill."

Montgomery gave Brandenburg the green light to go after Garnett, who was named one of the "10 greatest players in Wyoming history" during the program's centennial season in 2005.

"That's how the whole thing started," Brandenburg said.

During the next recruiting cycle, Brandenburg signed another big man from Regis, Mark Wrapp, and later added dynamic guard Mike Jackson from Aurora Central. Mark Engler, a 6-11 transfer from Minnesota, would be ready for the 1980-81 season. The intense, determined new Wyoming coach had quickly assembled a roster he believed was capable of making a run to the Final Four.

"Coach Brandenburg came to my house and said, 'I know you want to be a Wyoming Cowboy,'" Jackson recalled. "I was obviously very intimidated and treated him with tremendous respect. He just had that air about him, like you better fly in formation from the get-go. That's why were always so successful. He was very confident in how he presented himself, and my mother and father were very impressed with him and had a special place in their hearts for him."

Brandenburg's first season at Wyoming ended with a 15-12 record, but the Cowboys started to make War Memorial Fieldhouse as intimidating a place for visitors to play as Hell's Half Acre had been during Shelton's remarkable reign. The 1978-79 Pokes lost Brandenburg's first game, 71-56 to Oregon State in Laramie, but finished 14-2 on their home court, including a 71-69 overtime victory over NCAA Tournament-bound Brigham Young University. The season was capped off with a 70-65 win over Williams' Rams.

"It was great. One of the best times of my life," Irv Brown, the esteemed WAC referee who officiated at the Final Four from 1969-77, recalled of the atmosphere Brandenburg created in the Fieldhouse. "It was great theater. I once gave Jim Williams seven technical fouls, and we were still good friends. Brandenburg and I went back to his days at Aurora Hinkley. The man could coach. Brandenburg had the toughest matchup zone I've seen. They were really good."

Wyoming got off to an inauspicious start to the 1979-80 campaign with difficult losses to South Dakota (73-72) and Stanford (54-52) before rattling off six straight wins against inferior opposition. The Pokes also lost three painful WAC home games to UTEP (51-47), BYU (39-30) and CSU (51-49). The original game against the Rams in Fort Collins was postponed due to inclement weather, so the teams made it up on March 3, 1980, two days after CSU's win at War Memorial Fieldhouse.

"That first game in Laramie, I never even played," Jackson said. "I couldn't understand what he was thinking then. Now after coaching, I understand," said Jackson, who was a freshman that season. "We lost the game, and coach Brandenburg losing to CSU is not a good thing. Two days later he started me, and we won. I'm not saying that's the reason why we won, but ever since then I was kind of his point guard."

The Cowboys ended the season on a high note with a 67-64 triumph at Moby Gym to finish with an 18-10 record. There was no postseason berth for Wyoming, but it was clear to the rest of the WAC that this was a team on the rise. Earlier in the season, Brandenburg's young squad posted a 56-53 win in Provo, Utah, over BYU, which went on to win the conference and play in the NCAA Tournament. Jackson and Garnett were emerging as future stars while Bradley and Ollie already had the state engaged in the program again.

"Charles was a star and he carried himself like a star," said Wyoming associate athletic director Kevin McKinney, who was the team's young sports information director. "We were averaging 3,000 a night before Charles and Kenneth came along. They would come in before the game and they would actually stop and talk to people in those old bleachers. In my mind's eye I can still picture them both wearing suits. Kenny had like a tan three-piece, Charles wore coat and tie. They were incredible stars. Next thing you know there's 7,000, next thing you know there's 11,000, and we're winning the league after all those doormat years. They saved basketball at Wyoming. And Jim just kept getting pieces to go with those two."

Wyoming opened the breakthrough 1980-81 season with a 5-0 record, including an overtime win at Nebraska (62-59) in the opener and a 73-51 home victory over Stanford. The Pokes escaped the brutal San Diego State/Hawaii road trip unscathed to open the conference season. In the home opener Wyoming beat

UTEP 44-42, followed by an 85-54 thrashing of CSU in Fort Collins to get to 13-2 overall and 5-0 in the WAC.

"The rivalry with CSU was huge. You don't want to say hatred, but there was a dislike for the other players and that team," Jackson said. "I'm not even sure we respected them. Coach Brandenburg intensified that rivalry because he never wanted to lose to CSU, and that attitude carried down to the players."

After getting swept on the BYU-Utah trip, the Cowboys went 9-1 down the stretch to close out the season with the WAC title. The run included a 63-58 win in El Paso, a double-overtime victory over Danny Ainge-led BYU (86-84) and an equally tense 53-50 victory over Tom Chambers- and Danny Vranes-led Utah. The Cougars made it to the Elite Eight that season on Ainge's famous end-to-end drive and bucket to beat Notre Dame 61-60. The Cowboys were also invited to the Big Dance, ending a 14-year drought.

"It was unbelievable. The fans were on top of you in the Fieldhouse. They were only 15, 20 feet from the court. I know it only held 10,000, but it felt like 30,000," Jackson said. "We had 'The Freezer' section compiled of students holding the newspapers up while the other team was being introduced. That's a home court advantage right there. I'll always remember beating BYU and Utah back-to-back when they had Danny Ainge and Tom Chambers."

On March 6, 1981, Wyoming beat Air Force 46-38 at the Academy. The very next night the Pokes put an exclamation point on the regular season with a 97-70 thrashing of Jerry Tarkanian's UNLV team in Las Vegas.

"I thought we'd get killed against Tark's team because we had to come in the same day, have a shoot around, and then play the game," Brandenburg said. "And we beat UNLV by the largest margin they'd ever been beaten by in the old Convention Center. Our guys pounded their ass."

Wyoming opened the NCAA Tournament with a 78-43 victory over Howard on March 12, 1981, at Pauley Pavilion in Los Angeles. Bradley scored 20 points and Garnett added 18. Ollie had 10 rebounds. Two nights later in the second round, despite getting 25 points from Bradley and 15 from Garnett, the Cowboys lost 67-65 to Illinois. The Fighting Illini were awarded the decisive free throws in the final minute.

"That team was built for the Final Four," Brandenburg said of the 1980-81 Cowboys. "We had Illinois beat. We had them down three with less than two minutes left, and they called an offensive rebounding foul on Kenneth Ollie and they got a couple points there. Then they called a defensive rebound foul on Ollie and went to the free throw line again and made the free throws. The officials stole it; we were a better team. And once you get to that next round, there is no telling how far you can go."

Bradley led Wyoming in scoring as a sophomore (15.7 points per game), junior (19.1 ppg) and senior (19.2 ppg). He was drafted in the first round by the Boston Celtics after the 1981 season. He was a three-time All-WAC first team selection and was the program's leading scorer (1,744 points) upon leaving Laramie. Ollie also exhausted his eligibility that season. Brandenburg's promise of a conference title and an NCAA Tournament experience before they departed was fulfilled. Wyoming regrouped and went 7-3 against a formidable 1981-82 non-conference schedule that included only six home games, three Big Eight foes (Nebraska, Missouri, Colorado) and a neutral-court game against California The well-seasoned Pokes opened WAC play 7-1, including a sweep of BYU.

"You don't get good by playing a bunch of patsies," Brandenburg said. "When you first start the program you get some wins and confidence. But then you've got to play against some good teams."

During Bradley's senior season, Wyoming went 13-0 at War Memorial Fieldhouse. Meanwhile, construction on a brilliant new facility – the $15.7 million Arena-Auditorium – was well underway. The Cowboys had a 25-game winning streak in their old home snapped by UTEP on Feb. 13, 1982, in the Fieldhouse finale. A week later, Brandenburg's team opened the "Double-A" with a 59-29 victory over Air Force in front of a capacity crowd of 15,004.

"It's always great to come back to the University," Garnett told the "Laramie Boomerang" at the Arena-Auditorium 20-year celebration in 2002. "People here always make you feel special. I can't say enough, I love coming up here."

Wyoming finished the regular season with a three-game road trip, sweeping CSU (63-57), Hawaii (39-37) and San Diego State (66-64) to clinch a second consecutive WAC championship.

"We lost Charles and Kenny, but the rest of the guys were basically intact. We won the WAC by a record number of games.

We were fairly dominant that year," Brandenburg said. "Our last two conference games at Hawaii and San Diego we won very close games. It was always tough for us traveling to the West Coast and then all the way over to Hawaii. Jackson made a steal and laid it up late to win and saved the day against Hawaii. I think that won the conference. At San Diego State we didn't have a call go our way late, but Jackson hit a deep shot to win it."

Jackson said Wyoming was able to win 23 games that season against a difficult schedule because of the way Brandenburg prepared the team. He didn't waste time over-analyzing the opponent the way so many of today's coaches do in football and basketball.

"The thing that a lot of people don't realize about coach Brandenburg is we didn't spend a lot of time looking at film," Jackson said. "We spent a lot of time worrying about ourselves and what we do best."

On March 11, 1982, the Cowboys got the best of USC in the first round of the NCAA Tournament. Engler and Wrapp each finished with 17 points and nine rebounds to lead Wyoming to a 61-58 win over the Trojans in Logan, Utah. Dwight Johnson had 20 points in the first half before Jackson clamped down on the defense and held the USC star to two points in the second half. Brandenburg's tough team probably could have handled 90 percent of the field that season. Unfortunately for the Cowboys, a 7-foot legend in the making by the name of Patrick Ewing stood in the way of their Final Four dreams. Ewing, a 19-year-old freshman, intimidated Wyoming's usually unflappable veteran front line, and Georgetown advanced with a 51-43 victory.

"We had a sub-par game against Georgetown, and I'll take responsibility for that one myself," Brandenburg said almost 30 years later. "I knew they were going to play a 1-3-1 gap zone, and I thought we were prepared. I didn't do a good enough job preparing, and we did not play well. It was still the closest game Georgetown had on their run to the finals."

John Thompson's talented Hoyas, who were also led by Eric "Sleepy" Floyd, went on to blow out Fresno State (58-40) and Oregon State (69-45) en route to the Final Four. Georgetown beat Louisville in the national semifinals before losing 63-62 to North Carolina in one of the most memorable championship games ever played. Michael Jordan put the Tar Heels up by one point in the final seconds, and then Georgetown's Fred Brown mistook James Worthy for one of his teammates and turned the ball over.

Wyoming, despite Garnett's foul trouble, gave the Hoyas a good early test in the tournament.

"I can tell you I was intimidated at first. It took me a while to get out of my funk," Jackson said. "One of the Georgetown players took Garnett and threw him to the ground, and they called a foul on Bill. After that, Bill couldn't be as physical as he needed to be. Engler did very well, but as a team we did not play up to our potential. We played a little tentative and scared against them. I don't know what coach Brandenburg could have done about that. There is no one to blame."

"Brandenburg, Bradley, Engler, Garnett, Jackson, Ollie, Wrapp — when Wyoming fans think about the best of times at the old War Memorial Fieldhouse and the glory days of the WAC, these names immediately come to Mind."

"It's always very flattering. I still get people coming up saying, 'I remember you when you played,'" said Jackson, who went on to coach high school basketball in Wyoming and still lives in Cheyenne. "I think we had a special place in everybody's heart. We played the right way. I think if you're going to pick a team over the years to represent this community and this state . . . they can relate to us."

Garnett earned All-American honors after the 1981-82 season and was the number 4 overall pick in the NBA Draft by the Dallas Mavericks. Engler went on to play five seasons in the NBA with stops in Golden State, Milwaukee, Chicago, New Jersey and Portland. Jackson, an All-WAC first team selection in 1983, was drafted by the Kansas City Kings despite suffering a serious knee injury with three games remaining in his outstanding career at Wyoming. After posting unspectacular but winning seasons in 1983 (16-13) and 1984 (17-13), Brandenburg brought together another special group of players that college basketball fans not only in Wyoming, but around the country, still remember well.

"Something I will always be proud of is our two WAC championships, the teammates that I had, and coach Brandenburg got it all started," Garnett said.

The 'Dazzling' Dembo Days

Fennis Dembo.

The greatest name in college basketball history was literally the most "dazzling" player in Wyoming Cowboys' history, as the famous 1987 Sports Illustrated with Dembo on the cover attests.

"Of all the players that have ever played at Wyoming, I think Fennis was my favorite," said Bob Hammond, the Laramie Boomerang sports editor, who has covered the program for the local daily newspaper since 1964. "He was the kind of player that if you covered him or he was on your team, you loved him. But you hated him if you were the opposition."

Dembo and his twin sister, Fenise, received their unusual names at the suggestion of an older sister who wanted mom to stop at 12 children. The French word for "finished" is "fini." The story of the start to Fennis Dembo's memorable career with the Cowboys also required some creativity from Jim Brandenburg. The Wyoming head coach saw the lightly recruited prospect from San Antonio, Texas, where Brandenburg had also grown up, play at a high school all-star game in Waco, Texas, during the spring signing period in 1985. Brandenburg immediately envisioned the greatness other coaches were blind to and made a scholarship offer to Dembo.

"I talked to Fennis and he said, 'Well, Monday morning I'll be in the senior counselor's office at my high school at 10 a.m. Call me and I'll let you know if I'll come visit,'" Brandenburg recalled. "I thought this was just a great way to get rid of me. I thought the chances if him being there at that time were slim and none. But I called at 10, and he was there and agreed to come visit."

And then Brandenburg told Dembo to put his high school counselor on the phone. As luck would have it, Brandenburg had taught the woman at Burbank High School in San Antonio years before.

"Fennis made the trip up to Laramie. On the weekend he came to visit the skies opened up and it snowed and wind was blowing and everything else," Brandenburg said. "I thought that would probably not go well with him. But he enjoyed his trip and flopped on the ground and made snow angels and seemed to enjoy himself greatly . . . ."

"We couldn't get a plane out of Laramie, so we had to drive him in a snowstorm to Stapleton Airport (in Denver). The plane was delayed. We stayed with him there in the airport for hours and it was late in the evening when the plane left. I spent a lot of time with him and he told me he planned to come."

Brandenburg didn't hear from Dembo the next week and started to get nervous. He flew to San Antonio to see what was going on.

"I finally got a hold of (Dembo) on a Sunday night, and he said, 'Haven't you talked to my high school coach? My mom is going to get off work and I've got a press conference I'm going to hold. You can come by,'" Brandenburg said.

Dembo, foreshadowing the showmanship he would torment WAC crowds with in the future, announced that he was going to play basketball at the University of Wyoming. But why weren't major colleges lined up around the block trying to recruit this great athlete, skilled player and captivating personality?

"The reason was Fennis held everybody off and kept holding off his decision, so a lot of schools that had early interest in him dropped off of him," Brandenburg explained. "When I saw him in the all-star game, I was surprised he was still unsigned and then he committed to us. At about the same time, Kansas, Kentucky and all these schools started showing a little interest in him and it was just a little too late."

The overlooked Dembo turned out to be one of the most memorable players in college basketball history.

"The Southwest Conference was only interested in immediate impact players. They weren't looking for someone to help them down the line," Dembo said in the Sporting News' 1987-88 college basketball preview edition. The Cowboys' star appeared on the cover of the national publication. "Coach Brandenburg kind of let me develop my own personality on the floor. I grew two or three inches after I got to Wyoming and I got a lot stronger . . . . I never thought I was going to do this well. I just wanted to play and see what was going to happen."

Brandenburg, once again, saw something special that his peers were blind to.

"The first time I saw him, there was no doubt in my mind he could play," Brandenburg said. "It was like looking at Bo Derek and saying that's a fine-looking woman. It was pretty obvious."

UCLA had no interest in Eric Leckner. Neither did USC or California or Stanford. The 6-foot-11 prospect from Manhattan Beach, California, with soft hands and unlimited potential seemed destined to play college basketball for the Anteaters of UC-Irvine.

"I played at Mariposa High School in Manhattan Beach. We were in the Pacific Shores Conference and played Englewood and other inner-city schools. We used to get thrashed," Leckner said. "My senior year, I was getting letters from smaller academics like Rice and UC-Irvine . . . . I was not physically developed yet."

Leckner's high school coach, Jim Nielson, played basketball at Washington State in the early 1970s. At that time, Dennis Huston, one of Brandenburg's assistants at Wyoming, coached Nielson in Pullman. That connection led to a phone call from Nielson to Huston and a visit to Laramie for Leckner.

"I wanted to go to Wyoming from the start. I also visited Boise State," Leckner said. "UC-Irvine had (Tom) Tolbert and those guys; they said they would get my step-brother, we're the same age, into school; we could go there at the same time. So my family pressed me, and I committed to UC-Irvine. Everything was cool, but then after I signed they wanted me to go to summer school and redshirt as a freshman. I told them I didn't want to do it."

Back at Wyoming, Tony Martin, one of the most explosive and unheralded players in team history, was the Cowboys' star in 1983 and 1984. He led the program in scoring both seasons playing with Mike Jackson, Mark Wrapp, Dwight McClendon, Rodney Gowens and Anthony Johnson. But Brandenburg was still retooling and finished with a 33-26 record over those two seasons. Leckner called Huston over the summer to see if Wyoming's scholarship offer would still be on the table if he could get out of the commitment to UC-Irvine. On Aug. 25, 1984, UC-Irvine released Leckner and by Aug. 26, there was a new big man on the Laramie campus.

"On my recruiting trip I went to a game and Tony Martin was playing. It was freezing, and there were snowstorms. Tim Hunt was my host and he introduced me to college life and everything. I thought it was a perfect fit for me," Leckner said. "When I flew in to go to school, the first guy I meet is Dave Lodgins. He was a 6-10 freshman from Canada with a great shooting touch. So you don't really look at the team, you really just internalize your position. I just wanted to play.

"One thing about me is I just really want it more than anyone else."

With a little bit of luck and some deft closing skills on the recruiting trail, Brandenburg had suddenly signed a pair of stars that would shine brighter than the dynamic Charles Bradley-Kenneth Ollie duo, or Jackson and Bill Garnett during the dominant 1982 season. Lodgins was also a freshman and actually beat Leckner out for the starting job at center for the first eight games of that season. Mike Amundson, another skilled post, added quality depth throughout the next four seasons, along with Hunt. Brandenburg had also put together an impressive class the year before and wisely decided to redshirt point guard Sean Dent, shooting guard Turk Boyd and forward Jon Summers while the Cowboys transitioned from the back-to-back run of WAC championships.

"It was the perfect storm," Leckner said.

Wyoming assistant coach Dave Parker was in Houston looking at another prospect when he discovered Boyd.

"To be honest with you, it was culture shock. I had never been so far away from home," Boyd said of adjusting to college life in Laramie. "We had the number 1 fans in the country. They were so supportive of our team. Our team and the fans grew up together."

Sommers was more of a football prospect coming out of Evergreen (Colorado) High School, which is not surprising for Wyoming fans who fell in love with his physical play in the post.

"Wyoming started to recruit me after I went to Brandenburg's camp between my junior and senior year. They had a very successful program up there with Charles and Bill and Mark and those guys," Sommers said. "I wanted to stay in school along the Front Range. At the time, the CU and CSU football programs weren't good. So I kind of went along the basketball lines. Mark Getty took me around and I got exposed to Wyoming fans and the type of people that go to the University."

Dent arrived in Laramie all the way from Trenton, New Jersey, and decided to return home after his freshman season. He ended up going to a junior college for one season before making the most of a second chance with the Cowboys.

"It was different and I had a rough time my first year. I got really homesick," Dent said. "I had to redshirt because I didn't do well in school. I went to a juco (junior college) and I wasn't coming back. (A Wyoming teammate) Oliver Wilson talked me into that."

The young Cowboys finished just 15-14 during the 1984-85 season, those who were paying close attention knew this was going to be a special group of guys. Kevin McKinney vividly recalls a conversation between Brandenburg and Dembo on Dec. 10, 1984, in Lincoln, Nebraska, that set the tone for the next three years.

"I will never forget, we were at Nebraska and we had gone to practice and for some reason, either somebody wanted to interview Fennis after practice or something, but I drove Jim and Fennis back to the hotel from practice. The rest of the team had gone on the bus," McKinney said. "Jim sits in the back seat with Fennis and he goes, 'Fennis, I believe you are going to be a great player. You have everything that is needed to be a great player.' Now we had hardly seen him do anything at that point. And then Jim says, 'but you're going to have to do what I say to do. I'm going to have to break you down a little bit for that to happen because you're going to have to play better defense than you do, you're going to have to learn to shoot better from the perimeter than you do, but you do have the makings of a great player.' And then Jim said, 'Do you understand what I'm saying?'"

"I thought about that when Fennis was a great player. That was so much fun for me to see that happen. Of all the players – Flynn, Charles, any of our great ones that have weaved our tapestry – Fennis Dembo was to me the best. Because it was Fennis who turned it on when he got into the arena to make sure that every pound of pressure was on him."

Wyoming had wins over Colorado, Oregon, Baylor, Utah and BYU that season, but lost six of their final eight games, including a 61-60 loss to the Utes in the first round of the WAC Tournament. However, all of the experience gained by Dembo, Leckner and the rest of the freshmen would start paying off early. The Cowboys were 6-6 in non-conference play to open the 1985-86 schedule but got off to a 4-1 start in the WAC, including a 63-62 overtime win over conference favorite UTEP. Wyoming had a five-game winning streak snapped with a 74-72 loss at NCAA Tournament-bound Utah and then closed the regular season with a 65-62 win at BYU. The 1986 WAC Tournament was held at the Arena-Auditorium in Laramie. The Pokes used the home court advantage to pull off wins over Air Force (67-65) and New Mexico (56-54) before losing to UTEP (65-64) in the championship game with a berth to the NCAA Tournament at stake.

"We had the UTEP game won. They had missed a free throw, and Fennis got the rebound and they bear-hug tackled him. No call," Brandenburg said. "We had tied for the conference championship with UTEP and Utah. UTEP got the automatic bid, and Utah had their athletic director, Arnie Ferrin, on the NCAA selection committee, and they put them in the tournament. At the end of the year, we were playing the best. If we were playing Utah 10 times, we'd have won eight or nine. Even though I was upset with not getting the NCAA bid and believed the players deserved it, the run we made in the NIT was extremely good for us. Number one, because we had some great fan support."

The Arena-Auditorium was the place to be as Wyoming, led by 23 points from senior Les Bolden, beat Texas A&M (79-70) and then cruised by Loyola-Marymount (99-90) with Dembo scoring 24 points and grabbing 10 rebounds. Wyoming played with attitude and altitude.

"We were really blessed and drew great crowds, as the NIT gave us all home games until the finals," Dembo said. "We were a young team with many sophomores, so we just went out and enjoyed ourselves. Our fans were really supportive, and we grew up a lot."

With a trip to New York on the line, the Cowboys dispatched a really good Clemson team, which included longtime NBA standout Horace Grant, 62-57 in front of a capacity crowd.

"The one thing that stands out from all those games was just how packed the Arena-Auditorium was and just the excitement around town and how rabid the fans were," Sommers said. "When Fennis or Eric made a dunk, the place would just shake."

Dembo scored 19 points, grabbed 16 rebounds and then sat on the rim with his back against the backboard soaking in the celebration as the student body celebrated the victory over the Tigers on the court.

"I didn't know we were very good until we were in the WAC Tournament our sophomore year. That's when I knew we could beat anybody," Leckner said. "UTEP had (Dave) Feitl and those guys and they were a much better team at that point. But once we got to the NIT, nobody could have beaten us in the Double-A . . . ."

"The Clemson win will still go down as the most fun I've ever had on a basketball court."

Wyoming's memorable March run continued at Madison Square Garden with a 67-58 victory over Florida in the NIT semifinals. Dembo scored 23 points and Leckner grabbed 12 rebounds to outshine Gators' stars Vernon Maxwell and Dwayne Schintzius.

"We had kind of a verbal altercation on game day. We were trying to walk through some stuff in our shoot around. The Florida team came out on the floor and sat there right in the front row with their arms folded," Brandenburg said. "One of our coaches asked them if they would mind leaving. (Head coach Norm) Sloan hollered out and said, 'This isn't Hicksville, you're in the big-time now. It's open practice and we can stay here if we want.'

"We put it on them. It was one of the best defensive games Fennis Dembo ever played," Brandenburg said.

The Cowboys led Ohio State by 12 points in the NIT championship game before Leckner got into foul trouble and the deeper Buckeyes, led by Dennis Hopson's 26 points, won 73-63. Dembo scored 27 points in defeat and averaged 23.3 points in five NIT games. With a sophomore-dominated lineup, Wyoming was clearly a program on the rise and the WAC favorite going forward.

"The NIT was a tremendous development opportunity for those players," Brandenburg said. "They beat an ACC team, they beat an SEC team, and they played a tough Big Ten team dead even. They felt like they belonged and they could play with anybody."

Brandenburg had once again recruited and developed a group of players at Wyoming capable of making a run to the Final Four of the NCAA Tournament. Dent would leave the program as the all-time leader in assists and steals. Boyd is still remembered as one of the great athletes and role players to ever wear the Wyoming uniform. Sommers is still a beloved figure representing the toughness and spirit of the fan base. Leckner is easily one of the top 10 players in Cowboys' history. Dembo and Kenny Sailors are the two names most synonymous with Wyoming basketball.

"When you have a coach like Brandenburg, he kept saying, 'We're not there yet,'" Dent said. "We were getting there and we kept pushing and eventually it just started falling into place."

With high expectations on the high plains, Wyoming stumbled out of the gate during the 1986-87 season. Following home wins over Denver, Weber State, Idaho State and Colorado, the Pokes lost on the road at Texas Tech, Hardin-Simmons and Nebraska. The Cowboys also lost back-to-back WAC games against despised rivals BYU and Colorado State, which dropped their record to 8-5 overall and 1-2 in the conference.

"If you look back, we still had some bad games. Losing to Hardin-Simmons was miserable," Leckner said. "But that had nothing to do with Jim and the coaches. That was just mental. If the mental part of the game would have matched the physical part for our team, we would have been really dangerous."

On Jan. 10, 1987, Louisville – the defending national champions – made the trip to Laramie to test the Cowboys at the Arena-Auditorium. The Cowboys lost 67-64 but found their swagger. Wyoming would win 10 consecutive WAC games after nearly upsetting Denny Crum's top-10 team. Brandenburg's bunch still had some work to do at the WAC Tournament, however, after dropping their final two regular-season games at New Mexico and UTEP. Wyoming rebounded with a 56-54 victory over Utah in the opening round of the conference tournament, beat UTEP 77-74 in the semifinals and earned the automatic berth to the NCAA Tournament with a 64-62 victory over New Mexico at the Pit on March 7, 1987. In a 92-89 loss to the Lobos 10 days earlier, Dent was fouled in the waning seconds and missed two costly free throws.

"For me, the WAC championship game against New Mexico was probably the most important game I've ever played in because of the previous week," Dent said. "The next time I got fouled again and made the free throws, and we won and went on to the NCAA Tournament. Coach (Larry) Shyatt still gives me a little jabbing for that one. It was the most important game of my Wyoming career. If I don't make those, we probably go back to the NIT."

Shyatt, who began his second stint as the Wyoming head coach in 2011, was an assistant at New Mexico in the 1980s. The Lobos were the ones who settled for the NIT in 1987. BYU and UTEP received at-large bids, but Wyoming was the team with momentum and a purpose.

"We were inconsistent that year. Sometimes we would play really well, and other times not as well as I expected. But when it came down to the end at the conference tournament, we really started to come together at that point. I think we learned over a period of time that if we were going to make the NCAA Tournament we had to play our best basketball at the end of the year," Brandenburg said. "I always put a lot of offensive and defensive stuff in early and keep working on it, so we'd start to hit our stride in early or mid January. We did get better as a team and by the time we were in the conference tournament everything came together . . . ."

"We felt from the year before that we belonged and could compete on a national stage. That kind of set the tone for us. I can't remember what seed we had, but it should have been higher. There has always been a little bit of a bias from the NCAA Tournament committee when they start factoring everything in. There is an East Coast bias, but once you're under the big tent you just have to play."

Wyoming was a number 12 seed and opened the NCAA Tournament against number 5 Virginia in Salt Lake City. The Cowboys prevailed 64-60 in a game that wasn't as close as that score indicates. Leckner controlled the paint with 22 points, and Dembo had nine rebounds.

"We felt we were a better basketball team, and I was a little bit surprised that they were as tough physically as they were. They dished it out as well as we did. We were just a little bit better team than they were and won that game," Brandenburg said. "Later on I saw Dean Smith, and he usually compares everything in college basketball to what happens to North Carolina in the ACC. He sought me out and said, 'Jim, you beat a really good Virginia team.' That kind of caught his eye that we were pretty darn good."

The Cowboys advanced to face number 4 UCLA in the second round. The Bruins, led by Reggie Miller and Pooh Richardson, crushed Central Michigan in the first round and were likely thinking about a possible matchup with number 1 UNLV in the Sweet 16. They should have been focused on the dynamic Dembo and determined Leckner.

"I just remember how all we heard about was Miller. I recall so vividly (UCLA head coach) Walt Hazzard's press conference on Friday before the Saturday game. My brown and gold eyes and ears believed he was dissing us, that he was not totally sold on Wyoming," McKinney said. "It was like, 'We're UCLA, and he's Reggie Miller, and I'm Walt Hazzard. Fennis Dembo, good player. Wyoming, tough opponent.' But he didn't believe it. I remember sitting at that press conference thinking, 'You don't know how good Wyoming is.'"

Dembo was at his best, scoring a career-high 41 points to lead the Pokes to the upset over college basketball's most storied program. Miller scored 24 points but had to work for every single one of them against Sommers.

"Miller was on SportsCenter every night, so I had an idea that he was a great shooter and a good basketball player and all that. I was really unimpressed with the type of player he was," Sommers said. "He seemed like he had a lot of natural ability, but I wasn't very impressed with how he applied himself or his mental toughness. We got in his head and kept him off balance . . . ."

"Fennis was just on fire. Fennis is probably the best natural athlete I've ever seen in my life. He's just an incredible athlete and his skills really came out that game."

Dembo's scoring ability and showmanship highlighted Wyoming's 78-68 upset of the Bruins on March 14, 1987. He even won the verbal sparring match with Miller, who went on to have some famous wars of words with Spike Lee and the New York Knicks as a member of the Indiana Pacers.

"Hey, I've got no problem with that," Miller said in the Sporting News of Dembo's antics. "If you can back it up, do it."

The classic NCAA Tournament game between Wyoming and UCLA was in doubt until a last-minute spurt by the Cowboys that was punctuated with a breakaway dunk by Boyd. Suddenly, Dembo and the Pokes were the darlings of the NCAA Tournament.

"Usually when I'm playing, I'd count my points in my head. I'd try to keep up with my rebounds and all that personal stuff. But I knew we couldn't win that game thinking personal. I was just playing and trying to win the game. It really didn't dawn on me, how much I'd scored, until after we won and I saw the score sheet," Dembo said in a 2006 look back with Rivals.com. "When we got to Seattle for the next round, and I saw the reception I received from the fans at our practice at the Kingdome, that's when I started kind of saying, Oh, a lot of people were watching that (UCLA) game."

"During the news conference (before the UCLA game), Eric Leckner was from California and I guess he really had a vendetta. He was thinking he was better than Jack Haley, the center on their team. He was really jacked up about it. We were all pretty jacked up. He had a little extra motivation because he was from California and the Los Angeles area. When we had a press conference, Jack Haley was telling the news people and everybody, 'Hey, I'm the best center out here.' He was really looking forward to the challenge of playing against Jack Haley."

Dembo made the headlines with his 41 points, but Leckner was just as impressive with 20 points and 14 rebounds.

"Beating Virginia was great, but it was something I thought we would do. Beating UCLA, I personally carried that," Leckner said. "There was no letter from them, no call, they never respected anything about me. My family read the paper going into that game and it was obvious they were looking ahead to playing UNLV. The most fun I ever had was the win against Clemson, but my most gratifying win was UCLA."

UCLA had more stars. Wyoming had the brighter stars that day.

"UCLA was really talented. They had size and depth, but probably their nemesis was that they had three or four guys that thought they were the go-to-guy. I told our players that if the game was close in the second half, we were going to do it because they have two or three guys who think they're going to single-handedly win the game," Brandenburg said. "But we pretty much just handled them the whole way through. They kept going to Reggie Miller, and Miller would take Jon outside and do some isolation stuff. Then he would post up and ask for the ball back. He thought he was going to get the best of Jon around the block. Good luck with that one."

Wyoming basketball was back in the national spotlight. The Cowboys advanced to face number 1 UNLV in Seattle, just two wins away from realizing Brandenburg's vision of a Final Four. The Rebels, led by Armon Gilliam and Fred Banks, were even more of a Goliath than UCLA. Jerry Tarkanian's team was the favorite to cut down the nets at the Final Four that season.

"That year, Nevada-Las Vegas was number 1 in the country. And you had an Arizona team that was really good with Sean Elliott and all those guys. But quietly, we thought we were the best team in the West," Dembo said. "As a group we thought we were. We wanted to play the best teams in the West that were getting publicity, teams like UCLA, Arizona and UNLV. We wanted to see if our thoughts were (correct)."

The Cinderella Cowboys played a terrific first half and led UNLV by one point at the intermission. Leckner was in foul trouble. Gilliam finished with 38 points and 13 rebounds to lead the Rebels to a 92-78 win at the Kingdome on March 20, 1987.

"The next step in my maturation process was getting my ass kicked by Armon Gilliam," Leckner said of the great UNLV and NBA big man who died tragically of a heart attack playing basketball in 2011.

Dembo finished with 27 points and Leckner added 18. UNLV beat Iowa two nights later and advanced to the Final Four where Tarkanian's team lost to eventual national champion Indiana.

"(UNLV) had mature guys on their team with Freddie Banks, (Mark) Wade and (Jarvis) Basnight," Dembo said. "They were a very experienced group. I remember we were winning at halftime. I was celebrating as I walked to the locker room, and Mark Wade said, 'We've got one more half.' They just started wearing us down. They were more talented. We had a lot of talent, but that UNLV team was very talented."

The following season, all of Wyoming's talent was coming back. Brandenburg would not.

Great things were happening in the University of Wyoming's athletic department during the spring of 1987. The football team, coached by the legendary Paul Roach, was gearing up for back-to-back WAC titles. And the basketball program was coming off NIT championship game and NCAA Sweet 16 appearances with Dembo, Leckner, Dent, Boyd and Sommers all returning for their senior seasons. Brandenburg's Cowboys would certainly be favored to win the WAC, would be ranked in the preseason top 10, and had a chance to get Wyoming back to the Final Four. But on March 24, 1987, four days after the Cowboys' loss to UNLV in the Sweet 16, Brandenburg was introduced as the head coach at San Diego State.

"Totally stunned," McKinney said of the news. "There was a guy at the (San Diego) Union by the name of Ed Zieralski. Ed was covering the Aztecs and the league and he calls me late at night. I always felt like it was 2 O'clock in the morning, it was probably 10. He woke me up and said, 'I hate to call you at home, but Brandenburg is going to San Diego State.' I was half asleep and I go, 'Ed, don't do this right now.' He said, 'I'm not kidding you, I'm serious.' I said, 'There's no way Jim Brandenburg is going to leave these juniors to go to San Diego State. There's no way.' He said, 'I'm telling you it's going to happen tomorrow, be ready."

Roach, who was also Wyoming's athletic director, confirmed the stunning news that same evening to the San Diego Union.

"It's all over," Roach said in the paper after his counter-proposal failed to keep Brandenburg in Laramie. "He's on his way.

He's a hell of a guy, and he may get it done there. He met with his team, and he told them he was leaving."

Even the Aztecs, who had lost 25 of the 30 games before the hire, were surprised to lure a three-time WAC Coach of the Year away from Laramie. Only 836 spectators witnessed Smokey Gaines' last home game as the San Diego State head coach.

"I thought he was joking," Tracy Dildy, a San Diego State player in 1987, told the San Diego Union when a teammate informed him that Brandenburg was the next Aztecs' head coach. "He is such a great coach. He knows so many ways to win . . . . But I couldn't imagine him leaving Wyoming."

A quarter of a century later, many of the Cowboys understand Brandenburg's decision. They also can't help wondering what might have been had he stayed at Wyoming for 10 seasons.

"I think it was the best thing for Jim's family. As an adult I understand it," Leckner said. "As a junior losing in the (Sweet) 16 with everybody coming back, I did not understand it. And we didn't respond very well."

Even in 2011, Brandenburg did not want to get into all of the behind-the-scenes details of why he left what would have been his best team for massive rebuilding job at a program in the same conference. Brandenburg, a three-time WAC Coach of the Year at Wyoming, did explain his reasoning for accepting the San Diego State job.

"At the top of my list, I wanted to win a national championship. At the time, the NCAA was always talking about cutting spending and cost reduction and so forth. And because the recruiting in Wyoming is a little more expensive and expansive, I was worried that it would be harder to recruit and maintain a level of excellence. I thought getting to a metropolitan area would be in my best interest," Brandenburg explained. "When the San Diego State job opened, I misread that on several levels. I took the job with the promise of a new arena and thinking I knew what I could accomplish there. I went against all my basic principles as to evaluating a particular school, determining what they are and what they're not, and what is realistic and available at a school.

"I went to San Diego State thinking, one, I could run a freshman-based program like at Wyoming. I thought I would have a number of kids come up and develop a program that way. All of the evidence was there, and I didn't recognize it. It's a commuter-type school. I had made a mistake there. If I had looked at the history, even (Steve) Fisher now takes transfers, guys who were somewhere else and not happy, and juco kids. That's the kind of program San Diego State has been.

"Two, I thought in California I probably couldn't recruit the top-50 guys, because most of them would go to the Pac-10, but after the top 50 I could really compete. I was wrong there, too. We competed in the Mountain Time Zone and didn't get much coverage. San Diego was thought of in that time by Los Angeles and San Francisco kids as a leper colony for basketball. The few kids who did develop from San Diego County were influenced by shoe companies during tournaments in LA, and all of the agent runners had a great deal of influence on them. I misread who I could get and who I couldn't get. I probably had more attractiveness recruiting out of state. I also found a very limited budget and that the promise of a new facility was not on horizon."

In 1987, Roach was named Wyoming's athletic director and also coached the football team. Some of the basketball players at the time believe Brandenburg wanted to serve as the school's athletic director and head coach.

"It's kind of interesting when you look at that situation. How you view it now is different from when you are going through it," Sommers said. "There was a big struggle whether Wyoming would go football or put the emphasis in basketball. One big reason (Brandenburg) left is because he did not get the AD position and it went to Paul Roach. Basically, the University is saying we're going to be a football school, not a basketball school. Jim took the program from the cellar, to the top of the WAC, to a top-10 situation. From his perspective, I'm sure it was somewhat disheartening not be named AD."

The Wyoming players and administration knew there was a chance that Brandenburg would leave Laramie for a more high-profile job. It's something the athletic department had to deal with in football – Bob Devaney to Nebraska, Fred Akers to Texas, Dennis Erickson to Washington State – through the decades. But leaving for a down-and-out program in the WAC instead of waiting for a dream job to open up caught everyone off guard. Had Brandenburg stayed one more season and coached the 1987-88 Cowboys to their potential, he would have likely been in the mix for any opening in the country that spring. Instead, while struggling to gain traction at San Diego State, Brandenburg, who today lives in Austin, watched as Tom Penders was hired at Texas in 1988.

"I thought Jim's dream job was Texas," Leckner said. "It's somewhat ironic after our senior year the Texas job was available."

The Brandenburg era at San Diego got off to a promising start. The Aztecs upset 18th-ranked New Mexico and seventh-ranked BYU during the early stages of the 1988 WAC schedule. But after 11 consecutive winning seasons as a Division I head coach, Brandenburg's first San Diego State team finished the 1987-88 campaign 12-17 overall, including three losses to Wyoming (57-56 in San Diego, 85-59 in Laramie and 86-73 at the WAC Tournament).

"That spring they voted in a new arena, paid for by student fees, and I went to work on it with architects," Brandenburg said. "That's the arena they have right now. But it was held up for seven, eight years because people in surrounding community took it to court."

Brandenburg's Aztecs continued to play at the outdated Sports Arena in San Diego. Viejas Arena at Aztec Bowl, the beautiful state-of-the-art facility on the San Diego State campus today, was not completed until the summer of 1997. Steve Fisher, who won a national title at Michigan, was hired as the San Diego State head coach in 1999. It took Fisher 12 years to patiently build the Aztecs into a Mountain West contender and a Sweet 16 team. Brandenburg was 176-97 during nine seasons at Wyoming with four 20-win seasons, three NCAA Tournament appearances, and an NIT Final Four run. Previously, he was 39-16 in two seasons at Montana. At San Diego State, he was fired on Feb. 11, 1992, after losing 14 consecutive games and compiling an overall record of 52-87. Wyoming beat San Diego State 92-66 two days after Brandenburg received the pink slip from the Aztecs' administration and replaced on an interim basis by Jim Harrick Jr.

"Jim came to San Diego as a proven winner, but for whatever reason, he just didn't get it done," San Diego State athletic director, Fred Miller, said in the San Diego Union-Tribune of his decision to give up on Brandenburg. "The 2-19 record (at the time of the firing) was painful for Jim, painful to the team, and painful to the town. At that point, there came a time to make a change. He had five years. He had a fair shot at it. The success is not there. It's harsh, but that's the nature of this business."

Time heals all wounds. Jim Brandenburg still represents greatness at the University of Wyoming and would be on the Mt. Rushmore of great coaches at the school along with Ev Shelton, Devaney and Roach.

"Are you hurt by it? No. The guy gave us nine years of the greatest times we ever had," McKinney said. "You just wonder, why would he go there? And how good would Wyoming have been with those guys their senior year?"

Brandenburg still cares about Wyoming, too. He has been back to Laramie on a number of occasions, including for his induction into the University of Wyoming Athletics Hall of Fame in 2000, and remains in close contact with many of his Cowboys players.

"The Wyoming people and the University gave me a chance, and I'll always be grateful to them," Brandenburg said. "Right here in my office, I have an article about me and Ev. The article talking about me in the same breath as Shelton, as being great teachers, was a very kind compliment . . . ."

"If you look back at all those teams I had from early 80s to late 80s, I was blessed, and the University and fans were blessed with some of the finest young people I've ever coached or been around. These guys are still teammates and friends today with a great college education and experiences."

The Dome of Doom

Benny Dees was playing baseball and basketball at Brewton-Parker College in his small hometown of Mount Vernon, Georgia, when Lou McCullough, an assistant football coach from Wyoming under Phil Dickens, stopped by looking for athletes interested in playing for the Cowboys. Brewton-Parker did not field a junior college football team, but while driving through the South, McCullough was also keeping an eye out for baseball prospects that Wyoming baseball coach Bud Daniel might be interested in.

"McCullough was talking to our baseball coach, and Bud told him to find him a shortstop down here. Our coach said, 'I've got a guy who led our league in hitting and was all-conference and is going to take a low-major basketball scholarship,'" Dees recalled. "McCullough said, 'We'll take him.' I had never met coach Daniel until I got there."

Dees arrived in Laramie during the summer of 1958 and roomed with two football players from Georgia, who McCullough had also recruited to Laramie.

"Before coming to Wyoming, I had never seen the snow, never ridden on an airplane. There were a lot of things I hadn't done being a country boy from south Georgia," Dees said. "I was homesick and about ready to go home. Then one day Terry Eckhardt, who was on the basketball team, asked me if I played basketball. We went to the gym everyday. After we played for several days, I saw this impeccably dressed, silver-haired guy sitting in the corner. He would pull a chair up and just watched us from that corner. He did this for several days, and then one day he asked me if I'd come down to his office."

The gentleman was Ev Shelton. Dees lettered in basketball for the Cowboys in 1958, which was the legendary head coach's second-to-last season at Wyoming. Initially, Dees did play baseball for the Cowboys, who had made an appearance in the College World Series under Daniel in 1956.

"I thought Bud was really good. He was a good man, and I really learned a lot," Dees said. "But I was nothing to write home about as a shortstop."

Dees' best sport was basketball, but even during the lean years at the end of Shelton's remarkable run in Laramie it was difficult to crack the starting lineup. Tony Windis played the same position as the walk-on from Mt. Vernon.

"He had a great jump shot and he could take the ball to the goal. He was greatest finisher around the goal I've ever seen or played with," Dees said of Windis. "He had that two-handed overhead set shot. He was the only guy in the world that did that. (Eckhardt) was all-conference, also. So you know where I sat? Right beside coach Shelton."

Had Dees been able to play for Shelton from when he was a freshman, perhaps he would be known as much for his playing days in Laramie as he is for coaching the Cowboys later in life.

"The greatest compliment I ever had from coach Shelton, he taught a basketball class, and he said, 'If I had Benny Dees for four years, he'd be another Joe Capua,'" Dees said. "After graduating I could have stayed at Wyoming and coached the freshman team, but I was homesick for south Georgia and catfish."

Dees coached the Abraham Baldwin Agricultural College basketball team from 1962-67 and was the head coach at Virginia Commonwealth University from 1968-70. He worked as an assistant at Western Kentucky, Georgia Tech and Alabama before becoming a head coach again in 1985 at New Orleans, where he guided the Privateers to the NCAA Tournament in 1987. Led by Ledell Eackles, New Orleans beat BYU in the first round and lost to Alabama in the second round.

"New Orleans was not that tough a job. Of all the jobs I've had, including assistant at Alabama, New Orleans was one of the easier recruiting jobs I've ever had. The toughest was at the University of Wyoming," Dees said. "BYU had one of their better teams that year, too. We lost to Alabama, where I had been and recruited all those suckers, and they set an NCAA Tournament record for filed-goal percentage against us. They were good kids."

Shortly after the Privateers' season ended, Jim Brandenburg announced that he was leaving Wyoming for San Diego State. Charlie Spoonhour interviewed for, and was offered, the job in Laramie, but the Southwest Missouri State head coach passed on the opportunity to coach a ready-made NCAA Tournament team. Dees happily said yes to his alma mater, despite knowing he was Plan B.

"I was lucky to get it," said Dees, a longtime friend of Spoonhour's. "One night Charlie called me and said 'I ain't going to Wyoming, and you're their second guy.' I waited for them to call and took it."

Nearly 30 years after leaving Wyoming, Dees returned to coach a Cowboys squad that included Fennis Dembo, Eric Leckner, Sean Dent, Turk Boyd and Jon Sommers. Other talented players on the deep roster included Reggie Fox, Willie Jones, Robyn Davis, Dave Lodgins, Mike Amundson and Clauzell Williams. Expectations for the 1987-88 seasons rose high above Laramie's altitude of 7,220 feet. College basketball fans already knew who Dembo was after his magnificent March Madness performance the previous spring when the Cowboys beat Virginia and UCLA en route to the Sweet 16. He became a household name when *Sports Illustrated* decided to put "A Dazzling Dude" on the cover of its Nov. 18, 1987, college basketball preview edition. Here is an excerpt from Curry Kirkpatrick's scene-setting profile of Dees, Dembo and Company ahead of the campaign:

Laramie, Wyoming, might as well be Mars—it's such a desolate, gorgeous place. It's a special place, and this winter—if the cows come home, the winds stay clear, the snow doesn't white-out Benny Dees up to his own white hair and Dees, in his for-once serious words, "don't mess it all up"—Laramie may be the place to witness the finest college team in the land. And to think that until last March all anybody really knew about Wyoming basketball was the guy with a funny circus sideshow of a name.

Carrying Dembo's wild and woolly hot-dog reputation and now Dees's loose, homespun style as twin saddlebags, Wyoming is suddenly both a solid contender for the national championship and yet another reaffirmation of the ever-changing, crazy-quilt nature of college basketball. Who could have imagined that the national spotlight would land on a player and coach who represent a state with barely 470,000 inhabitants, 95 high schools and one lone member of the House of Representatives?

"Showboat, Hot Dog—I'll take any name they give me," says Dembo. "They're all compliments. The fans (on the road) love to hate me. But they don't want to do me no vitally harm. I fist 'em or talk back at 'em, and they got something to go home with. They're saying, Fennis did this and Fennis did that and Fennis heard us. I made their game."

"My biggest job is to keep the pressure off these kids," Dees said. "The state is piling it up. But we can be there when the dust settles. Maybe we'll need a last-second shot to keep going. But, hey, there aren't many times you get a chance to win the whole thing. Especially when you're in Wyoming. So, hey, we're goin' for it."

Obviously, right down to the Fennis . . . uh, finis.

Dees said his coaching career at Wyoming got off to a rocky start. During the first practice, Dees kicked Dembo out of the Arena-Auditorium to let the veteran team know there was a new sheriff in town.

"I was the happiest white man that ever lived when he was sitting in my office when practice was over," Dees said with a laugh. "We kind of laid down some rules. I did not mind him being as outgoing as he was, or what he said to the press, but you just gotta come to play. I'll tell you what, if he had not been in my office and left school, they would have lynched me. You would still be able to go to Laramie, look up and say, 'See all those bones? That's old Dees.'"

Most of the players embraced the gregarious Dees, who implemented an up-tempo style of play, which allowed the Cowboys to show off their athleticism and physically overwhelm most opponents, especially in the thin air on the high plains. And, at least initially, Wyoming picked up where it had left off in the NCAA Tournament under the more demanding, disciplined, and detail-oriented Brandenburg.

"When Benny came in, everybody on the team didn't know what to expect. Typically with Brandenburg, the first month was very challenging, physically and mentally, and somewhat exhausting," Sommers said. "Dees' first practice, everybody couldn't believe how easy it was. Eventually, that kind of showed."

The Cowboys opened the season with a 113-82 victory over Denver at the Arena-Auditorium and a 100-68 thrashing of Colorado in Boulder. Wyoming also beat Texas Tech (84-65), Alabama-Birmingham (74-69), Nebraska (87-58), Boise State (59-55) and Cincinnati (100-73) on the way to an 11-0 start and a top-five national ranking.

"We were ranked number 4 in the country. At that time, it was a lot of fun," Dent said. "But when you start having adversity, that's when you find out how you bounce back. And we went on a losing streak. Teams were gunning for us, and it wasn't easy playing in the WAC. When you have Fennis Dembo on your team, that makes Wyoming even more of a target on the road."

The Pokes were 0-2 in the WAC after losing at UTEP and New Mexico. After a win over Air Force, Wyoming fell to 1-3 in conference with a bitter loss to BYU. Eight days later, Dees – who had benched Dent in favor of Fox and Davis – was dealing with even more pressure from the fan base following a 54-49 loss at Colorado State.

"Those guys (Fox and Davis) were great athletes, but not having Sean as the starting point guard messed the nucleus up," said Boyd, who was Dent's longtime backcourt mate.

Wyoming escaped with a one-point victory over Brandenburg's first San Diego State team on Jan. 28, 1988, which began a stretch where the Cowboys won 13 of their next 14 games. When Brandenburg returned to the Arena-Auditorium as the visiting head coach on Feb. 27, the Pokes were starting to run on all cylinders again. Wyoming ran the Aztecs out of the gym, 85-59.

"Wyoming made a run at the start of the second half to break open a close game," *Laramie Boomerang* sports editor Bob Hammond recalled. "And Fennis runs by the San Diego State bench and yells to Brandenburg, 'Coach, you need a timeout.'"

The Arena-Auditorium was nicknamed the "Dome of Doom" during Dees' first season. The only loss Wyoming suffered over the last two months of the regular season was a costly 78-69 defeat at BYU. The Pokes responded with a Dent-led win at Utah to start a nine-game winning streak.

"The Utah game, I can remember Fennis ran up to coach Dees and said, 'If you don't get Sean in this game, we're going to lose,'" Dent said. "We started believing in each other again. We had already felt the pressure of being the hunted and we learned from it. We started to understand, everywhere you go, it doesn't matter where, they're after you. And we took the momentum right into the WAC Tournament."

Thanks to a sweep of the Pokes, BYU won the 1988 regular-season WAC title. That meant Wyoming would have to win the conference tournament on the Cougars' home floor, the Marriott Center in Provo, Utah, in order to be guaranteed a berth to the NCAA Tournament. Dees and the boys beat San Diego State 86-73 in the first round, with Fox scoring 19 points to lead the scoring. In the semifinals, the Cowboys, despite 24 points from Dembo, found themselves tied 58-58 with rival Colorado State with two seconds left on the clock. With his team inbounding the ball 94-feet away from the winning basket, Dees made a brilliant move by inserting the lanky Williams, a former all-state quarterback at Bedford High School in Detroit, into the game to throw the Hail Mary pass down court.

"It's our home-run play," Dees would tell reporters after the game. "And tonight we hit it out of the park."

Williams threw a John Elway-like pass to Leckner at the top of the key. The 6-11 center turned, released the shot, fell to the floor on his back, and looked up as the ball swished through the net as time expired to give Wyoming a 60-58 victory. Four years later, Grant Hill and Christian Laettner executed the exact same play to lift Duke to the famous 104-103 victory over Kentucky in the East Regional Final of the 1992 NCAA Tournament.

"It was *Leckner*, not Laettner. They've got that mixed up," McKinney said of the original play. "That's how it was going then. We were on top of the world . . . . At that point in time, that pass was going to be completed and that turn-around shot was going in. That's what happened to Wyoming at that point and time."

Wyoming also caught a break when UTEP beat host BYU in the other semifinal. In the WAC Tournament title game, Leckner scored 22 points and grabbed 10 rebounds to lead the Cowboys to a 79-75 victory over Tim Hardaway and the Miners. Dembo and his teammates were indeed dazzling. And dancing again. The struggles in January seemed to be a distant memory in March as Dees and the Pokes returned to the NCAA Tournament. But the excitement was short-lived as Wyoming, the seventh seed in the West, was upset 119-115 by Loyola Marymount in the first round on March 17, 1988, bringing a disappointing end to the great Dembo-Leckner days.

"We were trying to out-run-and-gun Loyola," Sommers said. "Under Brandenburg when we played them in the NIT, it was a lot different. In that game we took advantage of fast breaks when they were there, but the strategy was to make them tired guarding our half-court offense."

Despite getting 23 points from Leckner and 10 rebounds from Jones, Wyoming was unable to outscore Paul Westhead's Lions, as Bo Kimble scored 29 points and Hank Gathers grabbed 12 rebounds to lead the upset. Only Utah, which lost 127-120 in a four-overtime game in 1961, has ever scored more points than Wyoming's 115 in an NCAA Tournament game and lost.

"We should have beat Loyola Marymount by 30. What was their tallest player, 6-5? We should have slowed the system down and beat them by 30. But we wanted to run with Loyola Marymount," Leckner said. "I can tell you, I never looked past them or thought about playing North Carolina in the next round. That was the lowest point of my career. I thought we had the players to go head to head with anybody."

Even though Leckner's touches went down during his senior season in Dees' offense, his NBA draft stock stayed up. He was selected in the first round, 17th overall, by the Utah Jazz.

Dembo went in the second round, 30th overall, to the Detroit Pistons. Both Cowboys landed with good franchises, but for some reason Leckner and Dembo seemed to lack the drive to reach their full potential in the NBA. Leckner played eight seasons for seven different franchises. Dembo only lasted one season, but owns an NBA championship ring.

"I was not disciplined or motivated at the time, so I did not know what it took to be an NBA player," Dembo said during a 2010 interview with collegehoops.net. "I worked hard in college, but there is so much more discipline in the pros. There is no real training camp. You are expected to come in ready to play on day one, and it is a lot easier to get motivated when you are a starter in college than when you are sitting on the bench as a pro."

Dembo played professionally in Italy, France, Spain and Argentina. After his NBA career was finished, Leckner returned to Laramie to finish his business degree, paying his own tuition this time while grinding through 21 hours one semester and six more over a summer to earn the diploma.

"That's more important to me than being a first-round draft pick because it's real. I tie in my degree with the whole experience," Leckner said. "One of the things that happens is you're drafted at the time in your life when you are the least mature. In college, it's a team thing. You go to war with your team. In the league, it's all about you, the individual, and getting a contract.

"I can remember every single shot I took in the Clemson game and everything we did for six hours afterwards. I can't remember a single NBA game."

Dembo, Leckner and the rest of the group remain close friends. They frequently call, text or visit one another. Brandenburg remains an important part of their lives, too. Nearly a quarter of a century after taking Wyoming to the Sweet 16, the Cowboys of the late 1980s are still being talked about in Laramie. Dembo's jersey is still worn with pride at the Arena-Auditorium. While flattering, it's also a sad statement about the struggles the program has endured over the last two decades.

"What people need to realize is that what we experienced doesn't happen that often. Let that go. There are no more Fennis Dembo's out there. You can't wait for someone to be like Fennis," Leckner said. "Just go to the AA and enjoy the game. The best part of us, our team, is we loved the game. And the fans loved the game. We were just lucky to win, we were lucky to be a part of that team."

Boyd's son, who played college baseball, was channel surfing one night and came across a Wyoming basketball game on television. The Cowboys were down by double digits, and the announcers noted that the team had a lot of work to do to live up to the standard set by Dembo, Leckner, Dent, Sommers and Boyd.

"For me personally, when the tournament comes around I always drift back into the glory days. I always feel a little sentimental," Sommers said. "But it was such a wonderful experience with a fantastic group of guys. When you have a shared experience like that, you're always connected with these people. I'm very fortunate with that. It's good to know these people were still there and they will help you. They're like brothers, they really are.

The Benny Dees era at Wyoming really began with the 1988-89 season. With the loss of perhaps the greatest senior class in Wyoming history, the Cowboys started to rebuild with another talented crop of players that included Reggie Slater, Tim Breaux, Theo Ratliff, Queint Higgins, Maurice Alexander, Travis Butler, Michael Brown, Brian Rewers, Roman Totta, Reggie Page, Paris Bryant, Bobby Traylor and Steve Gosar. Despite Dees' accomplished recruiting skills, he never seemed to earn the trust of the fan base as a head coach.

"Benny was a quote a minute and all that. He was also a very good guy," McKinney said. "I felt bad for him because, and I don't care who it is, once you get a reputation you can't shake it. I remember one time we were in Hawaii getting some fast food after shoot-around, and Benny said, 'I've never been called a bad coach until I got to Wyoming.'"

"I have always been intrigued at the reputation coaches get when they come in. Some guys are behind the eight-ball, for whatever reason, before they coach a game here. Heath Schroyer never had a chance. Nobody liked Joe Tiller, an affable guy and a Wyoming guy through and through, but he followed Paul (Roach). No one liked Dana Dimel, and he was a very good head coach and did well here. And no one thought Benny could coach. Once Benny said, 'I could beat the Boston Celtics and there would be something wrong with it.' He always had that chip on his shoulder that people didn't like him here."

But they loved many of the Cowboys Dees lassoed to Laramie. None more so than Slater, a 6-5 forward from Houston, who became Wyoming's all-time leading rebounder with 1,197 boards from 1989-92, shattering Dembo's record (954).

"My mom was a teacher and when (assistant coach) Ray Thomas came down to recruit me he was a good salesman. He talked about the enrollment at Wyoming and the student-to-teacher ratio. They sold my mom," Slater said. "How they sold me was they had Fennis, Turk, Eric, Sommers . . . all those guys were leaving and it was a chance for me to play right away."

Wyoming finished 14-17 during the 1988-89 season but found a new star in Slater, who would be named All-WAC first team the next three seasons and honorable mention All-American as a senior. During the summer of 1989, the Cowboys added Breaux, a silky-smooth wing from Baton Rouge, Louisiana, who had attended a basketball camp at New Orleans as a sophomore in high school when Dees was the Privateers' head coach.

"When he had a break he allowed me to play pick-up ball with his players. Going into my senior year, he got the job at Wyoming and he always kept up with me and how I was doing and started recruited me," Breaux said. "Benny built a good relationship with my dad and we felt comfortable with him . . . . My junior year, they had gone to the Sweet 16. There was a lot of buzz about the program. Fennis was on the cover of *Sports Illustrated*, and that was a big part of me going there because it was a program on the rise."

No one who watched Slater and Breaux in action at the Arena-Auditorium was surprised later on when they played in the NBA. The most gifted prospect Dees lured to Laramie was Higgins, the1989 Alabama high school player of the year, who was recruited by Alabama, Georgetown, Louisiana State, North Carolina State and many other prominent basketball programs.

"He may be the best player we ever recruited," Dees said. "I still think about what would have happened to us if we had him to team up with Reggie as a senior, and then Queint and Theo together. Lord have mercy, we just would have been really good. It broke my heart to see what happened to him."

Higgins, who Dees described as "6-foot-9 and could run like a deer," averaged 8.5 points and 4.8 rebounds as a true freshman in 1989-90. The young Cowboys finished the season 15-14, but the pieces were in place to add more championship hardware to the trophy case in the years ahead. In the third game of his sophomore season, Higgins tore the anterior cruciate ligament in his right knee while attempting a dunk on a fast break at the end of a game Wyoming already had complete control of.

"I still remember the play like it was yesterday. I threw the ally oop to him," Breaux said. "We were a really talented team and thought we were definitely going to make it to the tournament."

Initially, the Cowboys recovered from Higgins' season-ending injury. The Pokes started 15-3 and were ranked in the top 25 after back-to-back wins over BYU on Jan. 19 (86-80 in Laramie) and Jan. 26 (77-72 in Provo) of 1991. But Wyoming lost seven of its final 10 regular-season games and settled for an appearance in the NIT. After a first-round victory over Butler at the Arena-Auditorium, Wyoming lost to Colorado in Boulder to finish 20-12.

"I always look back on that, and Reggie and I still talk about that, we just couldn't put it together for some reason," Breaux said. "We just had a lot of setbacks – Queint getting hurt or other guys being ineligible. But when I look back on it, wow, we had a lot of talent."

Ten months after his injury, Higgins suffered another serious knee injury during a fight at a party in Laramie. A third knee injury occurred in his first game back after recovering from the first two re-constructive surgeries.

"When I got to the locker room, I took off my shoes and socks and cried," Higgins said told the *Sporting News* in 1994. "I knew it had happened again. I wondered, 'Why me?' and questioned if I should go through it all again . . . ."

"I was worried all of the time about the knee. For two days, I started drinking – nonstop. I caught myself and called Theo and told him, 'This isn't me.' I went to drinking to forget, but it made me remember more. I love the game and it kept me going through the surgeries."

Just like Dembo and Leckner still wonder how history might have been different had Brandenburg stayed at Wyoming for their senior season, Slater and Breaux imagine what it would have been like playing alongside a healthy Higgins.

"When he came in, you had a guy that was a freshman that didn't have any hesitation, and made his presence known on the court. He played like a senior sometimes as a freshman," Slater said. "He came in there guns blazing. He was very athletic. I had to bring my game up because I can't have a freshman blocking my shots . . . . Even when I played in the NBA, guys would ask me: Whatever happened to Queint Higgins?"

Higgins played through pain and finished his career under Joby Wright in 1994. He graduated from Wyoming and later worked as the head coach at Laramie County Community College in Cheyenne. Higgins works as a counselor at the United States Sports Academy in Daphne, Alabama.

"(Higgins) is one of those guys, when you look at his skill set and ability, you think of Amare Stoudemire," Ratliff said. "Life takes crazy turns for people. You never know what is on your plate. He had all that ability and ended up having three knee surgeries. He was one of the top high school players in the country when he went to Wyoming.

Dees went to the rural Alabama well again in 1992 to recruit Ratliff from the small town of Demopolis. The tall, skinny kid had attended a summer camp at the University of Alabama as a junior, and then received a call from the Wyoming staff.

"Wyoming was the first Division I school that had interest in me with the expectations of me coming in to play right away. I looked up the school and found out what it was all about, and also looked at the roster to see who the big guys were and how many juniors and seniors they had," Ratliff said. "When I got to Wyoming I was 6-7, 160 (pounds). I was very thin. I had a lot of athleticism and I was just looking to come in and trying to get better. I didn't want to do that by sitting on the bench for two or three years, which would have been the case at bigger schools like Alabama."

Other than the temperature, Laramie reminded Ratliff of the comforts of home in Demopolis.

"I just went there and tried to have fun with my teammates and fell in love with the country," Ratliff said. "I didn't think it would be an adjustment with my lifestyle . . . . The snow, the blizzards and all that was definitely a culture shock. But it was a good time. I just wanted to maximize my opportunities there and get a degree."

Despite having three future NBA players in the starting lineup – Slater, Breaux and Ratliff – the Pokes were just 16-13 during the 1991-92 season. "Mo" Alexander usually viewed himself as the man in the offense. On February 9, 1991, Alexander set an Arena-Auditorium record with 49 points. Wyoming lost the game to New Mexico, 85-83, when the shoot-first point guard turned the ball over on the last possession of overtime.

"I thought Benny Dees was a good coach," Slater said. "He had a lot of hats to wear – disciplinarian, encourager, coach, friend. I thought we were very talented, and it was just a matter of self-discipline. There are two types of coaching disciplines that I think of. The first are the coaches who treat you like the army or the armed services, where you have superior officers who bark out orders at you and you follow them and have no choice. The second are like Benny Dees and some other coaches, where they give you rope, and if you are a self-starter you can shine like crazy. But if you need them to bark orders, they're not going to do much with that rope. Benny gave guys rope, and unfortunately some of us hung ourselves with it."

The Cowboys were 13-15 in 1992-93, which led to a coaching change. Dees was 104-77 in six seasons at Wyoming with two 20-win seasons, two mediocre seasons, two losing seasons, one NCAA Tournament appearance and one NIT appearance. Only four men who have coached the Wyoming basketball program for at least five seasons – Willard Witte (.724), Shelton (.620), Brandenburg (.645) and Steve McClain (.577) – had better winning percentages than Dees (.575).

Dees decided to beat the posse out of Laramie, leaving before the speculation that he would be fired became a reality. He was the head coach at Western Carolina from 1993-95 before finishing his career as a high school coach in his native Georgia. Dees' son, Josh, is an assistant at the College of Southern Idaho. They coached the program to the National Junior College Athletics Association national title in 2011. Josh Dees walked on at Wyoming, where he was a ball boy when Benny was the head coach, before finishing his playing career at Western Carolina. Gosar, a Pinedale native, was a reserve guard for the Pokes from 1991-93.

"Josh is a really good recruiter," said Dees, who spent a month in Idaho watching his son and Gosar coach.

Joby Wright was hired to replace Dees prior to the 1993-94 season. Bob Knight recommended the former Indiana star and assistant coach to Wyoming athletic director Paul Roach. Although the program needed some discipline, the transition was not an easy one for Ratliff, who initially considered an Alabama transfer.

"Benny is a great guy. He's a very funny guy and a serious guy at the same time. I remember spending the holidays at his house with his wife, Nancy, and his kids were real young at that time. We enjoyed each other's company. He was a definitely a good coach and a good recruiter," Ratliff said. "It was tough at first not knowing the situation we were going to be in. Coaches came to my house trying to pull me back to Alabama. I thought it would be a great chance to play in front of my family with some great teams. But going through the interview process, we had a chance to meet with Joby, and I had a gut feeling he would be great for me and the team. I think for me as a defensive-minded player, his Indiana background and his background as a defensive player were good for me. He told me all I needed to do was work on certain parts of my game and my dreams of playing in the NBA or overseas would be fulfilled. And he was right."

During Wright's first two seasons, the Cowboys went 27-29. But Ratliff shattered Wyoming's all-time blocks record, finishing his career with 425 blocks (Leckner previously owned the record with 164 blocks) and was named All-WAC first team as a junior and senior. He was drafted in the first round (18th overall) by Detroit, led the NBA in blocks three times, started for the Eastern Conference in the 2001 All-Star Game and recently completed a 16-year NBA career with the Los Angeles Lakers after stops in Philadelphia, Atlanta, Portland, Boston, Minnesota, San Antonio and Charlotte.

"Once I got into the league, I knew I could play in the league. Before the draft, I had a chance to go back to Demopolis and spend time with my family. Being the 18th pick was a dream come true. Every guy who plays, dreams of playing in the NBA, and taking care of their family. Especially when you grow up in a poor area and your family has to work so hard. It was an early Christmas present," Ratliff said. "To be from a small town in Alabama and to have played at a small school like Wyoming . . . to be in this position is amazing. Every place I played, I took a life lesson. I met so many people in so many cities and across the world. It definitely altered my life."

Ratliff said the 2010-11 season was his last in the NBA. Despite never playing in a postseason tournament at Wyoming, he never regretted his decision to go to school in Laramie.

"You don't think about the basketball stuff. It's more about the people you hung out with," Ratliff said. "I remember the people more than the basketball . . . the guys on the team and the classes we took. I still keep in touch with a lot of my teammates."

After finishing his career at Wyoming, Breaux was playing in a pick-up game in Houston when a scout for the Rockets discovered the undrafted gem prior to the 1994-95 season. He was invited to training camp and caught the eye of head coach Rudy Tomjanovich.

"The scout kept coming to the gym that summer and then going back to Rudy and saying, 'We've got a kid who can help us. There's no one our team who can get to the basket like this guy,'" Breaux said. "Chris Jent had to have a knee scoped, and instead of doing it right after the season, he waited until that July. That opened up a spot for me on the summer league team."

Breaux was signed to a contract and was suddenly teammates with: Sam Cassell, Robert Horry, Kenny Smith, Otis Thorpe, Clyde Drexler and Hakeem Olajuwon. The Rockets won their second consecutive NBA championship that season.

"That was something that at the time when it happened, it took me a couple years to make it to the NBA; I didn't really understand the magnitude of making a championship team undrafted," Breaux said. "Looking back, it was a wonderful opportunity to play with Hakeem and Clyde and win a championship."

Breaux played three seasons in the NBA, spent quality time with three different CBA franchises, and also played professionally in Spain, Turkey, Italy and Germany until retiring from basketball and getting into the mortgage industry in 2005.

Slater, who led Wyoming in scoring in 1990 (16.7 ppg), 1991 (19.2 ppg) and 1992 (17.9 ppg), played eight seasons in the NBA with Denver, Portland, Dallas, Toronto, Minnesota, New Jersey and Atlanta. The "Big Cat," as he was nicknamed with the Cowboys, was on the verge of stardom with the Nuggets before suffering a knee injury. He owns six automotive shops and a gym in Houston, where Breaux also lives and works. After Heath Schroyer was fired at Wyoming during the 2010-11 season, Slater was a part of the athletic department's search committee for a new head coach.

"I was honored that the University thought so much of me to be involved. It was a very interesting day and process to sit there and listen to what people on the board had to say about what we needed," Slater said. "Here's something that will maybe answer that question of whether or not Wyoming can get it back. In 1991, we played and defeated Butler. That was 20 years ago. We were at the same starting block; in fact we were little ahead of where Butler was. When you look at Butler and Wyoming they aren't that different."

Butler, of course, played in the NCAA national championship game in 2010 and 2011, losing to Duke and UConn.

"In that sense, I think any devoted college can get to where they need to be," Slater said. "It can be like the Dembo era and beyond."

'I Still Get Cold Shivers'

Marcus Bailey was born and raised in Cheyenne. His father, Henry, played basketball for Bill Strannigan and Moe Radovich from 1972-74, and his uncle, Craig Shanor, played for the Cowboys from 1974-76. As an impressionable kid in the late 1980s, Bailey got caught up in the excitement of the Fennis Dembo-Eric Leckner era and dreamed of putting on a Cowboy jersey some day.

"To me, and I think a lot of people in Wyoming, those guys are like our Michael Jordan and Larry Bird and Magic Johnson," Bailey said of the Wyoming stars who compiled 74 wins, two NCAA Tournament appearances and a trip to the NIT title game from 1985-88. "Fennis Dembo was like the greatest basketball player in the world to me. Those are my earliest memories of the program, going to see Fennis and Eric play."

Bailey clearly had a knack for the game, but he was one of the shorter players on the Cheyenne East High School team until a growth spurt that began his junior year. Bailey was the 4A (the largest classification in Wyoming) player of the year as a senior in 1999, averaging 28.4 points per game and leading East to a third-place finish at the state tournament. Despite the accomplishments, there were no Division I offers on the table for the late-blooming 6-foot-5 wing. In fact, the Colorado School of Mines, a Division II program that plays in the Rocky Mountain Athletic Conference, was the only program to make Bailey an official offer. He reluctantly accepted an academic scholarship at Wyoming believing his playing days were over.

"I was frustrated because I didn't think anyone realized how good I could be," Bailey said. "And no one had really talked to me."

Wyoming head coach Steve McClain and his assistants followed Bailey's impressive prep career. The staff had an open scholarship during the spring signing period in 1999 and decided to see if the local boy could make good in the Mountain West.

"We knew Marcus was a really good player, and I still remember the day we brought him over and offered him," McClain said. "Did I know he'd be as good as he ended up? I'd be lying if I said I knew he would be that good. We did know how important it was to have an in-state kid who was also a really good player."

Bailey rewarded McClain right away, emerging as a starter during his freshman season and helping the Cowboys finish with

19 wins, averaging 7.8 points, 3.4 rebounds and shooting 51.5 percent from the field in 31 games.

"I was kind of just expecting to grow as a player and get bigger and stronger and ride the bench for a couple years. I thought maybe I'd be a role player my junior and senior year," Bailey said. "I was surprised when coach McClain was putting me on the first team right away in practice. He said he was going to play me right away. All that experience really paid off the next couple years."

In the fall of 2000, the Wyoming football team suffered through a miserable 1-10 season under first-year head coach Vic Koenning, who finished an ugly three-year reign in Laramie with five wins and 29 losses. McClain's talented lineup and an aggressive, up-tempo style of play, gave fans something to cheer about. The Arena-Auditorium was rocking again, and Bailey's number 44 jersey was flying of the sales rack. The Cowboys got off to a 7-1 start in Mountain West play during the 2000-01 season and finished in a three-way tie with BYU and Utah for the conference title. If the Pokes didn't get swept by UNLV – a heartbreaking 80-78 buzzer-beating loss in Laramie and a wild 106-102 loss at the Thomas & Mack Center – they could have been the outright champions and likely punched a ticket to the NCAA Tournament. Instead, the disappointed young group went through the motions in the opening round of the NIT and was beaten at home by Pepperdine in the opening round, 72-69.

"A very disappointing year, and I still think about it because we were a year older and we had a great group of players," said Bailey, who earned All-Mountain West first team honors after averaging 17.4 points and 4.1 rebounds as a sophomore. "We had a group of players and a team that was NCAA Tournament-caliber. But we had some bad losses. That was probably my best individual year, but also my most disappointing year. I would have rather have had team success."

Bailey and the Cowboys would bounce back in a big way, restoring a much-needed shine to the once proud program.

Wyoming was the first school Josh Davis visited during the recruiting process, stopping in Laramie on the way back to his hometown of Salem, Oregon, from an AAU Tournament. He also considered Gonzaga and California State Northridge before committing to first-year Cowboys' head coach Larry Shyatt. Before Davis enrolled, Shyatt left Wyoming for Clemson.

"It never really crossed my mind," Davis said when asked if he considered transferring after Shyatt's abrupt departure. "I made a commitment to the University. I was just excited to go there. It was a good place for me."

McClain, a fiery 35-year-old who had coached Hutchinson (Kansas) Community College to a junior college national championship before mentoring under Billy Tubbs at TCU, was hired as Wyoming's new coach. He was aware of the program's history, dating back to his playing days in neighboring Nebraska at Chadron State.

"I knew it was a great opportunity for a young head coach. I knew what the culture was. I knew what Jim Brandenburg had done there," McClain said. "I also knew the program had been down for a while and it was a great opportunity to change that. We came in with the idea of playing up tempo and using the altitude to our favor. Even though early on we weren't as talented as some other teams, we used the altitude to wear them out."

During McClain's first season in Laramie (1998-99), Ugo Udezue, whose season-high as a freshman was 12 points against Air Force, averaged 20.5 points per game in the new system to lead the Cowboys to 18 wins. Wyoming beat USC in the opening round of the NIT and then lost at Oregon, a bittersweet homecoming for Davis.

"It was wild, kind of helping turn the program around as a freshman," said Davis, who averaged 8.6 points and 6.0 rebounds that season with an eye-opening 22-point, 13-rebound performance against number 13 Arizona. "I had a lot to learn and I needed to gain a lot of weight and get bigger. But to start as a freshman was incredible, and beating USC was one of the most memorable games of career. Playing Oregon was rough, not much of a welcome home."

In addition to Bailey, Davis and Udezue, Wyoming's roster entering the 2001-02 season included steady point guard Chris McMillian, highly-touted freshman Jay Straight, clutch shooting guard Donta Richardson, Iowa State transfer Paris Corner, and powerful center Uche Nsonwu-Amadi. Unfortunately, Udezue missed the 1999-2000 season due to a serious knee injury and was never the same player. And over that summer, the veteran McMillian suffered a serious leg injury playing softball, which forced the baby-faced Straight to lead the team and altered the chemistry. The Cowboys struggled early with the NCAA-Tournament-or-bust expectations. The Pokes were dealt head-scratching road losses to Detroit and Boise State in non-conference play.

"Because of Chris' injury, I was slightly apprehensive. Marcus probably was too with a freshman point guard and a different style," Davis said. "Danta was coming in as a juco shooter, so we had to change our whole look around. But we were just so talented from top to bottom. I still wish that Chris could have been with us though. We lived together, he was my boy, and we had a connection on the court."

After a loss to Bobby Knight's Texas Tech Red Raiders in Lubbock on New Year's Day, the Cowboys responded with a 5-0 start to conference play, including road victories at UNLV (69-59) and San Diego State (88-85, overtime). Entering the regular-season finale, Wyoming and Utah were tied atop the standings with 10-3 records. The Cowboys beat the Utes 57-56 on March 2, 2002, to capture the program's first outright conference championship in 16 seasons.

"It was an unbelievable environment and something I can remember to this day," McClain said. "It had been so long since Wyoming had won a championship, and to do it on that floor for fans that drove four hours and made that sacrifice was special."

The Arena-Auditorium seats 15,028 people. The official attendance for the Wyoming-Utah title tilt was 16,089. Just about everyone who witnessed the game stayed to watch the team cut down the nets. The scene was reminiscent of Dembo sitting on the rim after the Cowboys' beat Clemson in the NIT to advance to the Final Four at Madison Square Garden.

"It was insane. They packed over 16,000 in and it was standing room only. I don't know if it was Fire Marshall legal or not," Davis said of his final home game. "My family, and fiancé, who's my wife now, were there. It was an incredible experience."

Bailey made two free throws in the final seconds to give Wyoming a four-point lead.

"I remember usually being able to keep my emotions in check and not getting nervous. In that moment, I was nervous. When I looked at my hands during a timeout, they were shaking," Bailey said. "I don't even know what was said in the huddle. I was just thinking, 'If you make these free throws, we're going to win the conference championship.'"

Bailey came through. The game was not quite over. Utah's Nick Jacobson splashed a 3-pointer at the buzzer, Corner ran at the sharpshooter and nearly fouled him. The official swallowed the whistle, and Wyoming escaped with the one-point victory.

"Paris shouldn't have been in the vicinity (of Jacobson). As soon as I made the free throws, we could have cleared out and let them score. We should have sat on floor," Bailey said. "Paris couldn't even enjoy the victory. I still talk to him, and he has never gotten over it."

The Cowboys entered the Mountain West Tournament as the number 1 seed but still had a little work to do to secure an at-large bid to the NCAA Tournament. In the first round, Air Force, which had never won a conference tournament game, was leading Wyoming by three points as time was about to expire in regulation. The Pokes had survived a four-overtime thriller to beat the Falcons 83-76 in Laramie and escaped Clune Arena with a 51-48 win during the regular season. This time Bailey started the March madness early with a 3-pointer, which forced overtime and allowed the Cowboys to win, 69-67, for their 21st victory of the season.

"That was a scary game. I hated playing Air Force," Davis said. "There is no other team I hated playing more than Air Force. Every single game I played them, I dreaded it. It was their style of play, the players they had on the team, it was just rough every game. The shot Marcus hit was a life-saver. I don't even want to think about what might have happened if we lost that game."

Wyoming did lose in the quarterfinals, 70-69 to San Diego State, which forced the team to sweat out their postseason fate on Selection Sunday. The Cowboys were the last at-large team revealed during the live unveiling of the bracket. And their match-up with Gonzaga drew a lot of national attention because the Bulldogs were ranked number 6 in the polls but given only a number 6 seed in the West Regional.

"The best position to be in as an athlete is playing a game where you have nothing to lose and everything to gain," Davis said. "There was no pressure. We were relieved that we made it to the NCAA Tournament. It was serendipitous."

Davis had 11 points and 14 rebounds in the game against Gonzaga. He also put together one of the best end-to-end highlights in program history, throwing down a dunk on one end and rejecting a layup attempt by All-American Dan Dickau on the other to deliver a 73-66 upset of the Zags in the final minute at The Pit in Albuquerque, New Mexico.

"I don't think we're a Cinderella," McClain told reporters after Wyoming's first NCAA Tournament victory since Dembo scored 41 points in the win over UCLA in 1987. "I think we're a team with a purpose."

The Cowboys, despite their number 11 seed, had the look of another team capable of making a run to the Sweet 16.

"It did feel like it. Josh had the follow-up dunk and then blocked Dickau . . . that clip is one of that I'll still watch on Youtube," Bailey said. "He was a beast during that tournament. He almost played like a possessed individual. It was his last hurrah and he put everything out on the floor."

Davis had 17 points and 11 rebounds in the second round against Arizona, but it wasn't enough to overcome the best game of Luke Walton's college career (21 points and nine assists) as the Wildcats advanced with a 68-60 victory.

"Luke Walton had an unbelievable game, and they shot 28 free throws and we shot four," McClain recalled. Actually, Wyoming took seven free throws and made four. "I'll never forget when we walked down the ramp at halftime of the first game and the crowd just erupted."

After the game, McClain said of the run: "We established that Wyoming basketball is going to be around for awhile."

With Bailey, Nsonwu-Amadi, Richardson and Straight, all returning, the 2002-03 season looked promising. But dark clouds were headed for Laramie once again.

McClain never received the credit he deserved for putting Wyoming basketball back in the spotlight. Fans harped on the fact that Shyatt had recruited Davis before leaving and made the assumption that Nsonwu-Amadi was an easy recruit because he was Udezue's cousin. There was also a misconception that any coach would have noticed Bailey's potential coming out of Cheyenne East. The truth is, McClain is as fantastic recruiter. In later years, he did make some recruiting mistakes, and attrition in the program was a factor in his dismissal after nine seasons and a 157-115 record. But 40 years after Strannigan began pulling great players out of Illinois, McClain brought some dynamic players from the Windy City to Laramie.

"(Straight) was the one that started it. We went in there and started recruiting him, and I asked Bill Self (the Illinois coach at the time, who is now at Kansas if he was going to offer him. Bill said he'd be a great player at Wyoming," McClain said. "The job we did on the court with Jay and the academic job we did with Jay sold Justin Williams and Brandon Ewing. Sometimes kids are your best recruiters."

Straight was an all-State player at Chicago's Dunbar High School and led the Chicago Public League in scoring as a senior, averaging 29.8 points and 7.0 assists per game. He was named co-freshman of the year in the Mountain West after running the offense on Wyoming's talented NCAA Tournament team. He was honorable mention all-conference as a sophomore, second team as a junior, and first team as a senior. Straight was ranked as one of the top-15 point guard prospects coming out of high school and chose Wyoming over Boston College, Iowa State, Marquette, Notre Dame and St. Louis. He finished his Wyoming career with 1,550 points (11th in program history), 453 assists (third) and 161 steals (seventh). Straight has played professionally in Germany, Greece, Poland and the NBA's Developmental League.

"We knew Jason was a huge recruit from Chicago and we played with him on his visit. We could tell he was going to step in and fill that void when Chris got hurt," Bailey said. "Jason's a good athlete and smart on the court. He was very impressive as a freshman. I think it might have been his best year as a pure point guard because he knew he had juniors and seniors around him."

After earning his degree in 2005, Straight passed the torch to incoming freshman Brandon Ewing, an even more touted recruit from Chicago's Julian High School. The Pokes also welcomed Justin Williams, a Theo Ratliff-style shot blocker. The pressure was starting to mount on McClain after an 11-17 finish in 2004, a 15-13 finish during Straight's senior season in 2005, and a 12-17 record entering the Mountain West Tournament in 2006. Before play began in the conference tournament, McClain said: "I may be gone, I don't know," when asked about speculation that athletic director Gary Barta was going to fire him when the season concluded. Ewing, dynamic guard Brad Jones, and Williams were spectacular at the Pepsi Center in Denver as the seventh-seeded Cowboys upset Air Force in the opening round and Utah in the semifinals. Williams posted a triple-double – 10 points, 15 rebounds and 12 blocks – in the win over the Utes, which advanced Wyoming to the championship game against San Diego State. The Pokes were about to be fitted for a glass slipper as a most unlikely Cinderella at the NCAA Tournament, leading the Aztecs by four points with 2:18 remaining in overtime, but Brandon Heath took over from there to lead San Diego State to a

69-64 victory and the automatic berth. Ewing scored 22 points to close out an impressive freshman season.

"I have a very good memory about that game. We knew the situation we were in. We really wanted to get to the NCAA Tournament for coach McClain and all the seniors," Ewing said. "Towards the end of the year, everybody finally got healthy and we made a good run."

Despite spectacular individual play by Ewing, the only four-time All-Mountain West honoree in the league's history, it would be as close to the Big Dance as he would get. Wyoming finished with a winning record (17-15) in 2006-07, but new athletic director Tom Burman decided it was time to try something new and fired McClain.

"Looking back on my last three years, individually I did a great job. I'd take all those stats away if I could go to the tournament with my team," Ewing said. "I wish we could have given Wyoming what they're used to seeing with Marcus Bailey, Josh Davis, Jay Straight and even back to Fennis Dembo."

Ewing finished a remarkable career second on Wyoming's all-time scoring list behind Dembo with 2,168 points. The three-time Mountain West scoring champion was also second on the conference's all-time scoring list behind Heath until BYU's Jimmer Fredette shattered the record in 2011. Additionally, Ewing graduated as the Poke's all-time leader in free throws made (697), free throws attempted (855), 3-pointers made (193), 3-pointers attempted (594) and games started (126). He is second behind Sean Dent in assists (471) and third behind Dent and Dembo in steals (161). Ewing could have gone to DePaul, Louisville, Marquette or Purdue coming out of Chicago.

"The coaches did a great job recruiting, and making me feel like family," Ewing said. "I had a great time there. Chicago's called "the Windy City." I think Laramie is the real Windy City."

Ewing has had a successful professional career since graduating from Wyoming in 2010, playing in Israel and Greece. His NBA dreams are still alive after leading the Cyprus League in scoring in 2011.

"Before I went to Wyoming, I knew about Jay Straight and Justin Williams. I knew about Fennis Dembo because of the *Sport's Illustrated* article," Ewing said. "I knew who Theo Ratliff and Reggie Slater were from the NBA, but I didn't know they went to Wyoming. Those things came to me as I walked around proud to be a Cowboy."

Wyoming basketball has gone through its share of difficult times over the decades, and the program has seen more than its share of star players suffer career-crippling injuries. But the most devastating, momentum-killing night in the history of the Arena-Auditorium was on Dec. 19, 2003. The Cowboys were coming off a successful appearance in the Great Alaska Shootout and a payback victory over Knight and Texas Tech when South Carolina arrived for a rare SEC appearance in Laramie. The Cowboys were crushing the Gamecocks when Bailey stole the ball and went up for a dunk late in the game. As soon as the All-American candidate came down on the floor, everyone in the building knew Wyoming's homegrown hero was in trouble.

"I had been playing on a bum ankle since the Alaskan Shootout. But we had beaten Texas Tech when they were in the top 25. Going into the South Carolina game, I talked to the radio guys for the pregame show and told them once this game was over I was going to take at least a week off," Bailey said. "I had favored the other leg so much that my knee kind of just buckled gave out on me. I felt it hyper-extend, but at first I didn't think it was going to be anything serious. The doctor did the test right there and he told me when I was on the ground that I was done."

Bailey, who scored 19 points during the 77-63 victory over South Carolina, suffered a torn anterior cruciate ligament. It was Wyoming's ninth game of his senior season, which made Bailey ineligible for a medical hardship by three games. The Cowboys still finished with 21 wins and made it to the second round of the NIT, where the season came to an end against North Carolina in Chapel Hill. There is no doubt in the minds of Bailey, McClain, or anyone associated with the program, that the injury dramatically changed the course of history.

"I still get cold shivers when you say it," said McClain, who became Jeff Bzdelik's top Colorado assistant, and then Tom Crean's at Indiana after leaving Wyoming. "There's no question in my mind we would have won our third straight Mountain West championship. That team would have went into the NCAA Tournament capable of making a deep run with Marcus."

McClain said a third Mountain West title would have made things easier in recruiting. They wouldn't have experienced as much of a drop off after the graduation of Davis and Bailey.

"To have to sit there in street clothes and watch your best friends, who are almost like your brothers, was very hard," Bailey said. "I don't think it would have been as hard if it were my sophomore or junior year. I tried to help out when I could. I'll admit, I just didn't feel the same. At that age, basketball becomes serious at that level. I had plans to play professionally and to play for a long time. To have it end that abruptly is hard to accept. There was a change in my mood and emotions. It was rough for two or three years."

The 2003 draft was one of the best, at least at the top, in the NBA's history with LeBron James, Carmelo Anthony, Chris Bosh and Dwayne Wade all being selected in the top five. Moving down the list, UNLV's Marcus Banks went off the board at number 13. That's about the range Bailey was being projected to go by some scouts before the injury. He competed at a couple of NBA training camps after healing from surgery but never made a roster. And the thoughts of what might have been for the Cowboys and his NBA career were hard to shake.

"A little bit of depression just hit me and I ended up withdrawing from classes that semester I was hurt," Bailey admits. "I could never get the knee 100 percent and I tried to go back to school, but I didn't enjoy it."

Bailey, who is a Mormon, went on a church mission in Germany in 2005 that changed his perspective.

"I went to Hamburg and that was a great experience. That was when I finally got over what happened and was able to move on, just because I was so involved in service and helping and learning a language and doing something meaningful," Bailey said. "At that point, I was really able to not forget it, but at least accept it and move on."

Bailey returned to Wyoming in 2008 and finished his undergraduate degree. In 2008-09, he played professionally in England. Although he was still able to dominate, the knee never felt quite right.

"I had a good season but I made a decision not to keep doing this to my body," Bailey said.

In 2011, Bailey was back in Laramie taking science classes while applying at medical schools.

Davis, an All-American at Wyoming, continues to live the hoops dream. He has made several stops in the NBA (Atlanta, Philadelphia, Toronto, Milwaukee, Houston and Phoenix) and enjoyed successful stints playing in high-level professional leagues in Russia and Italy.

"I still hang out with Marcus in the summer. He's one of my best friends," said Davis, who makes his home in Golden, Colorado, when he's not working overseas. "I can't complain about playing basketball to pay the bills. There are a few of us that are still doing it. It's definitely become a job now, but it's a lot of fun. My 5-year-old and 2-year-old have been to more countries than most people ever go to."

Shyatt Happens . . . Again

Heath Schroyer talked a great game after replacing Steve McClain in the spring of 2007.

"I know how important this program is to the state of Wyoming, and to Cowboy fans throughout the country," Schroyer said after being hired by Tom Burman as the 20th coach in the program's history. "It is my belief that this job has unlimited potential. It is a special place."

Schroyer was fired just shy of four years later with seven games remaining in the 2010-11 season. His record at Wyoming was 49-68, including a dismal 16-41 mark in the Mountain West. Like Benny Dees, Schroyer's best season was his first one as the Cowboys finished 19-14 in 2008 with an appearance in the College Basketball Invitational. Despite inheriting one of the conference's top backcourts, the duo of Brandon Ewing and Brad Jones, Wyoming was a non-factor in its own conference and drawing just over 4,000 fans in the cavernous Arena-Auditorium. New Mexico hired Steve Alford at the same time Burman went after Schroyer, who he had also hired at Portland State while serving as that school's athletic director. The Lobos posted a 98-39 record in Alford's first four seasons with four postseason appearances.

"I can't pinpoint a real factor why Heath struggled so much," said Ewing, who played two seasons for McClain and two seasons for Schroyer. "After the Steve McClain era, the people put a lot of pressure on Heath to compete with the past."

McClain led Wyoming to one NCAA Tournament, two Mountain West titles, and three NIT appearances in nine years. Schroyer, an assistant under McClain in 2001-02 when the Cowboys went to the Big Dance and upset number 6 Gonzaga, wasn't able to accomplish a lot, other than improving the team's sagging Academic Progress Report numbers. A 102-78 loss to BYU in the Cougars' final home game as a member of the Mountain West was rock bottom for the Cowboys. Wyoming finished the 2011 campaign with 21 losses and ranked 256th nationally in points per game (65.9), 294th in rebounds per game (32.4) and 322 in assists per game (10.5).

It was time to call an old friend for help. Burman, whose search committee included associate athletic director Kevin McKinney and former Wyoming star Reggie Slater, made a bold decision to hire Larry Shyatt as the new head coach on March 31, 2011. The same Larry Shyatt who former athletic director Lee

Moon hired and then sued when he left Wyoming after one season (1997-98) to take the Clemson job.

"In this day and age, there are no warm and fuzzy stories in sports. It's all about crooks and cheating. But that is why we're back here, because it's the right thing to do," Shyatt said. "We're always telling our recruits to do the next right thing. For the next 10, eight, six years, until they run us out, this is the next right thing to do."

Gregg Sawyer played basketball in Burns, Wyoming, a town of about 300 people located about 25 miles east of Cheyenne, not too far from where Kenny Sailors invented the jump shot on a farm near Hillsdale. Sawyer's father, Ron, was the head coach. Sawyer earned 12 varsity letters in football, basketball and track for the Broncs. Wyoming head coach Joby Wright wisely recruited Sawyer to play for the Cowboys. The 1994 graduate had envisioned himself playing in front of sold-out crowds at the Arena-Auditorium like Fennis Dembo and the boys in the late 1980s.

"I grew up in a gym. I aspired to play college basketball, even in fifth or sixth grade," Sawyer said. "That was a big reason why I wanted to be a Cowboy, I remember watching (Sean) Dent, Dembo and (Eric) Leckner play. And they packed house."

Benny Dees watched Sawyer shred the competition at the state tournament during his sophomore season. Wright stayed on the trail after getting hired before the 1993-94 season. The first-year Wyoming coach, who had been an assistant at Indiana before being hired by then athletic director Paul Roach, even attended a game in Burns and spoke at Sawyer's senior banquet.

"I will forever be grateful to Joby. He took a chance on me, a Wyoming kid," Sawyer said. "He was old school coming from Bobby Knight. It was a real learning experience and made me a better player."

Wright guided the Cowboys to a 14-14 record in 1993-94, his first season. Sawyer arrived the next season and played sparingly as the Cowboys continued the define mediocrity with records of 13-15 and 14-15. In 1996-97, Sawyer started every game, but the Pokes finished 12-16. Despite inheriting Theo Ratliff and recruiting some skillful, physically blessed players, including La-Drell Whitehead, David Murray, Jeron Roberts and HL Coleman, Wright couldn't get the program back in WAC contention. Moon fired Wright in the spring of 1997 and brought in the personable, highly respected Shyatt, who was Rick Barnes' top assistant at Clemson, to get the program back on track.

"Joby had some great athletes he recruited into the program. I don't know why it didn't work out better. The only real comparison I have at that level was coach Shyatt my last year," Sawyer said. "For some reason, (Wright) couldn't get every single person to buy in. We had some talented teams. And they're all good guys and I'm friends with them to this day. It was rewarding and a lot of fun to have some success with Shyatt as a senior."

Shyatt was happening in Laramie. The Cowboys opened the 1997-98 season with five consecutive wins, including a 62-58 victory against Colorado in Boulder, and were 10-2 during non-conference play. Shyatt quickly reestablished the Arena-Auditorium as a place where nobody would push the Pokes around. Without inheriting any all-conference talent or depth, Shyatt was able to lead Wyoming to upset of New Mexico and Utah when both teams were ranked in the top 10. Rick Majerus' Utes made it all the way to the national championship game that season.

"I can remember those last few games when we upset Majerus' fourth-ranked Utah team, and two nights later beat a pretty good BYU team," Shyatt said. "Our crowd . . . they were loud and as challenging as any fans I had seen. We did not do very well with our people early that year, but as we won a little, and maybe earned their respect, it became an intimidating facility."

Sawyer averaged 14.4 points, 3.2 rebounds and 2.2 assists as a senior. Wyoming finished 19-9 and lost to Gonzaga in the opening round of the NIT. With an 18-7 record and a top-40 RPI entering the WAC Tournament in Las Vegas, the Cowboys were perhaps only one victory away from the NCAA Tournament. But Sawyer missed an open jumper in the final seconds, and San Diego State escaped with a 60-57 victory in the first round.

"I was just talking to coach Shyatt about that the other day. I had a 15-footer with four seconds left. It was right there," Sawyer said. "But I do remember some of those games that season and the mindset that coach Shyatt instilled. Talent-wise we were down, and coach knew we weren't going to be able to run up and down the floor. He molded around what he had, and we played defense. The mindset we had defensively was to not let the ball get into the paint. It was just a real team-oriented defense. Everybody bought into his philosophy. People had roles and they followed them."

Barnes left Clemson that spring to take the Texas job. The Tigers' administration lured Shyatt back to South Carolina before his first full recruiting class at Wyoming, which included Josh Davis, ever stepped on campus in Laramie. Shyatt coached at Clemson for five years and then spent seven season as the associate head coach at Florida under Bill Donovan, helping the Gators win three SEC title and the 2006 and 2007 NCAA national championships. Wyoming and Shyatt kissed and made up 14 years after their memorable first date.

"I always said I wouldn't consider another head coaching job unless it was somebody that knew (my wife) Pam and I well, and was somebody that we trusted and knew well. So that passes the first major litmus test," Shyatt said. "It wasn't until I sat down with (Wyoming president) Tom Buchanon, Tom Burman, and their committee that I really considered it. They were so honest about where we are. They said, 'We're hurt, we're broken, it doesn't look the same as when you were here. The crowds are gone, we've lost our love affair with the fans . . . we'd really like you to come back if you're interested in making us competitive again.'"

"It was a breath of fresh air, not just their honesty, but the fact that, unlike most people, they didn't want to win last year's national championship. They simply want to win back the respect and the competitiveness and the spirit. When I got home, Pam said, 'Why wouldn't we? You've always been about challenges. We were never happy with the way we left before, whether we did right by our children or not, we were never happy about it.'"

With most of his belongings still packed in boxes and littered throughout his old/new office, Larry Shyatt made a discovery when interviewed for *Cowboy Up*.

"We won a national championship?" Shyatt said when told about Kenny Sailors. "Jeremy, get in here."

Jeremy Shyatt was in the 11th grade during his dad's first stint at Wyoming. His brother Jeff was in the eight grade, and his brother Phillip was in the sixth grade. Now Jeremy is a member of the new coaching staff.

"It's every coach's dream, but especially every father's dream," Larry Shyatt said of working with his oldest son. "In our line of business, when you're gone 150 to 175 days a year and miss so many things, you find it hard to make up that time. This is a blessing. He's also a pretty talented coach, but for me it's a blessing to get to work with him."

The state of Wyoming, for the most part, seems to have forgiven Shyatt for leaving after one season. There hasn't been this much excitement surrounding Cowboys basketball since the 2002 NCAA Tournament. The old "Shyatt Happens" T-shirts the students wore in 1998 were flying off the rack after his reintroduction press conference.

"It's incredibly unique. I didn't think he would do it to begin with. But I am impressed that he is honorable enough to tell us at least that he wanted to finish the job that he didn't complete. That's all you have to say to me, a Wyoming guy," said McKinney, who has been working in the Wyoming athletic department since 1967. "I've always hoped that guys would stay as long as they could, knowing they won't. One year is pretty tough. It has happened to us twice, (Dennis) Erickson (in football) and Larry. Both of them showed us a little window of what we were going to be and then they went away. Fortunately, Paul (Roach) kept the window open after Erickson left. After Larry left, we weren't what we could have been, or at least in my mind what I envisioned we would be with him.

"Larry has a great ability, and I've only seen this one year now, to make his players play just like we are – hard-nosed, blue collar, against the world, not a lot of ability. Wyoming people, I think we have abilities in some things, but we will always out-work you. We may not have more ability than you, but we will out-work you, and we're tougher than you are. That's how our mentality is. If you say, Well, you are a great rancher. The answer is, Oh, I wouldn't say that now. But I'll out-work you and I'll spend more time out there than you will. But I don't really think I'm a great rancher."

"We don't like to be told that we're great, we just want to be appreciated for our work ethic and our ability to get it done. That's how Larry does it."

Shortly after taking the job, Shyatt reached out to Dembo and a number of other great Cowboys.

"The fans and the boosters and the students at the university cannot wait for Wyoming to go to the (Sweet) 16 and then buy tickets. That's fake. Go and support the team and the new coach and see if they get better from one game to the next," Leckner said when asked about Shyatt. "When I was a freshman in 1984, there was no Internet, no Facebook, no tweeting. If you wanted to know what was going on at the basketball game, you went to the game . . . . They're lucky to have that guy. Let's just support him and go see if they're playing better the next game."

After Shyatt was told about the 1943 NCAA championship trophy and Sailors' glory days, the coach figured out that the old guy he had met at the press conference in the suites at War Memorial Stadium was the jump shot inventor. The light bulb immediately went on above Shyatt's head.

"Jeremy, let's put something on this wall that says, 'Wyoming, national champions,'" Shyatt said. "Something for the recruits to see."

At Wyoming, tradition can take a few years off. And as Shyatt's rehiring symbolizes, it also returns.

"I'm hopeful I'm here for all the right reasons, and that when we leave here we're competitive and we do have a spirit about us and a program the people of Wyoming are prouder of," Shyatt said. "Those are the goals that I have."

Shining Star of a Storied Program

The Cowboys' NCAA championship run was almost blown off course by the winds of war. On Nov. 10, 1942, university presidents at a number of rival institutions, most notably the University of Colorado, voted to cancel their 1942-43 basketball seasons due to World War II. Wyoming President J.L. Morrill and the University's faculty athletic committee issued this statement:

The announcement by the Colorado college presidents probably anticipates what is inevitable for colleges and universities in this war emergency. Travel restrictions and the forthcoming lower draft age doubtless will make it impossible to conduct any normal program of intercollegiate athletics. Wyoming believes it right an proper for the Colorado institutions to meet the situation as they see fit, and the Colorado decision is accepted without criticism or complaint by our University.

If it is necessary to discontinue intercollegiate athletics, the University of Wyoming will gladly comply. Meantime, it is our hope and intention to undertake the eastern basketball trip, which has been scheduled late in December, and to decide jointly with other members of the Mountain States Intercollegiate Athletic Conference at their regular December meeting, the future status of our athletic activities in this region.

The Cowboys would provide a wonderful escape from the hardships of wartime for basketball fans from Laramie to Long Island, finishing with a 31-2 record (10-0 in conference) en route to the NCAA title and a victory over NIT champion St. John's at Madison Square Garden.

During the glory days of the old Mountain States Conference, which is also known as the Skyline Conference and was referred to as the "Big Seven" by fans and media at the time, Colorado and Wyoming had one of the nation's best hardwood rivalries. The Buffs were coached by the legendary Forrest B. Cox, who compiled a record of 147-89 at Colorado from 1936-50 with four conference titles. The Cowboys' Hall of Fame coach, Ev Shelton, racked up eight conference crowns from 1941-58 and had a 328-201 record during 19 seasons in Laramie. Ironically, Cox, whose nickname was "Frosty," is credited with giving Half Acre Gym in Laramie the "Hell's Half Acre" nickname.

"They were tough," Wyoming All-American Kenny Sailors said of the Colorado teams from his era. "Cox hated to come to Half Acre. He just didn't want to play Shelton here. He said, 'I'll play you anywhere, I just don't want to play in Half Acre.' He's the one that called it Hell's Half Acre. He's the one that named that place. I don't think we ever lost a game to Colorado in there."

Colorado and Wyoming both burst onto the national scene after capturing the attention of East Coast basketball fans and media in New York. In 1938, the Buffaloes played in the first National Invitation Tournament at Madison Square Garden, beating New York University in the semifinals and losing to Temple in the title game. Cox's crew won the Mountain States Conference that season, but not without suffering a 44-39 loss at Hell's Half Acre. In 1940, the Buffs, following a rare sweep of Wyoming during the regular season, were the stars of Broadway after beating DePaul in the semifinals and Duquesne in the championship game to win the NIT.

"That happened every year in those days," Bob Kirchner, a member of Colorado's great teams in the early 1940s, said of the program's non-conference and postseason excursions to the Big Apple. "That was just a normal trip for us. I don't remember ever losing a game back there."

As Colorado prepared for its historic trip to New York, the *Boulder Daily Camera* documented a heated skirmish with the Cowboys in the paper's March 8, 1940, edition:

> *The pinnacle for slam-bang roughness came in the Colorado-Wyoming game in Boulder when the Cowboys up from Laramie way decided to try a little football stuff on the hardwood. Blocks such have seldom been shown by a Wyoming football team came into play, and it looked for a time like the two clubs would have to start using a huddle and get out their shoulder pads to finish the game. But no riot broke out, and the Herd trampled the Punchers, to prove that sound basketball is better than roughhouse tactics anytime.*

During the 1940-41 season, Wyoming swept the series on the way to its first Skyline Conference championship. In 1941-42, Colorado won the conference with an 11-1 record (16-2 overall), ascended to number 1 in the national rankings, and advanced to the NCAA Tournament. The Buffs were led by All-Americans Robert Doll and Leason McCloud, and their home court, Balch Fieldhouse, had every bleacher seat filled during this golden age of basketball in Boulder. Colorado opened the season with a lengthy road trip to the East Coast. The team wore suits, ties and Fedoras while traveling across the country by train. It all started with a 45-29 trouncing of St. Joseph's in Philadelphia on Dec. 27, 1941. The ships in Pearl Harbor were still smoking 20 days after the infamous Japanese attack. Three nights later, the Buffs beat St. John's 39-33 at Madison Square Garden. The New York writers were fascinated with the personable Cox and his well-oiled CU machine. After easy wins over St. Bonaventure (52-28) and Loyola-Chicago (57-43), the Herd headed home. The Buffs dispatched Utah 49-39 in the Mountain States opener on Jan. 9, 1942. CU was off to a 14-0 start following a 52-35 thrashing of BYU on Feb. 28. The team's only loss of the regular season was a maddening 40-39 defeat against Wyoming on March 3.

"That was a great team they had. I remember the only game we lost was in Laramie by one point," Kirchner said. Colorado did beat Wyoming 59-53 at Balch Fieldhouse on Jan. 24, 1941. "We played ball control, there was no shot clock. They had Jim Weir and Sailors and (Milo) Komenich. I was impressed. Ev Shelton's teams had a lot of class . . . ."

"That one game we lost, I believe I'm right that we turned the ball over once," Kirchner recalled. "And Wyoming didn't have a turnover."

Colorado regrouped and beat Utah State on the road four days later to secure another conference championship. The reward? A trip to Kansas City, to face Kansas in the NCAA Tournament. Those who followed the Big 12 Conference through black and gold glasses are painfully aware that the mighty Jayhawks won the final 18 meetings with Colorado, which officially left for the Pac-12 Conference on July 1, 2011. Kansas leads the all-time series with Colorado, 122-39. That trend started early as the Buffs lost five of the first six games against Dr. Forrest C. "Phog" Allen's teams in the early 1930s. But this was a different brand of Buffs. Colorado upset the Jayhawks 46-44 to advance to the national semifinals (only eight teams, four from the West and four from the East, were invited to the not-so Big Dance at that time).

"We liked that," said Kirchner, who grew up in Topeka, Kansas. "Kansas had one of the best teams they ever had at that time, too. Frosty had been an assistant under Phog Allen, and most of us were from Kansas. What an experience."

The journey ended two days later as the Buffs fell 46-35 to Stanford. The Cardinal went on to beat Dartmouth in the national championship game. The fighting around the world loomed over one of the greatest basketball seasons in Colorado's history.

"We thought about it as much as we should have been," Kirchner, the only known surviving member of the team, said of the war and the inevitability of joining the fight. "That time, 1941-42, was the beginning of the war and things weren't as unsettled as they got to be later as the war wore on. So many of our good friends were enlisting and off to training. We didn't lose any from the basketball team. At least not that year."

Colorado did not play basketball during the 1942-43 or 1943-44 seasons due to the war. Most of the players were drafted and began serving before they could even celebrate the accomplishments of a 16-2 season. Some of the Buffs gave the ultimate sacrifice for the country. Kirchner's senior season was wiped out, but he was on the Denver Legion team that gave the Cowboys one of their two losses during Wyoming's championship run in 1943.

On Dec. 7, 1941, nervous young University of Wyoming students, who would become a part of the Greatest Generation, listened in stunned silence to the radio reports. The Japanese had attacked Pearl Harbor, and the news stopped everyone in their tracks at the Student Union on campus.

"You could buy a Coke for a nickel in the student union, and a good ham sandwich went for 20 cents," Hall of Fame sports writer Larry Birleffi, a student at Wyoming during Sailors' era, once wrote. "The winds of war were changing, and just about everybody waited for the call. But something else was happening on the Wyoming campus. . . ."

"Nobody could have dreamed what was ahead for this team. A ticket to Hell's Half Acre became tougher to get than a new four-ply retread."

And so the greatest show in basketball continued. Wyoming began the 1941-42 season on Dec. 20 with a 47-34 victory at Montana. Over the next two years, Shelton's Cowboys would compile a dominant 46-7 record, including a 12-game winning streak and a 23-game winning streak. The 1942-43 campaign was capped off with the 31-2 record, the NCAA championship, and the exclamation point victory over NIT champion St. John's at Madison Square Garden.

"We thought about the war quite a bit. We all knew we were in," Sailors said. "I was already commissioned a second lieutenant in the Marines on a regular commission. I knew I was going to be heading to the South Pacific because they told me. But they did let me finish the year."

About 10 days after the Cowboys returned home from New York as conquering basketball heroes, and in possession of the national championship trophy, Sailors – who had been named the NCAA Tournament's Most Outstanding Player – was headed to Quantico, Virginia, for training. Teammates Floyd Volker and Jimmy Collins joined Sailors at the Marine Base. Jimmy Weir did not return to Laramie after the St. John's game, instead reporting directly to the Army post in Fort Benning, Georgia, as a second lieutenant in the infantry. A total of seven members of the 1943 NCAA title team served in the military during World War II. Collins never made it back home, a casualty of the war. Wyoming reluctantly canceled the 1943-44 season. The Cowboys would help defend the country but would not have a chance to defend their national championship.

"These fine young men will soon be in the armed services," president Morrill said at the team banquet in Cheyenne in April of 1943. "Who doubts victory there?"

A house ad in the *Laramie Daily Bulletin* bragged of the Cowboys with a headline: **Welcome to the World's Champions of Basketball . . . The Wyoming Punchers**

The subtext read: *The same spirit that took the Cowboys through the NCAA meets at Kansas City and New York City and enabled them to win at Madison Square Garden last Thursday evening, is the spirit that will spell victory for our country in her biggest game of history.*

Sailors, Volker and Collins were sent to San Diego before having to face combat overseas. They all played together on a stacked military team, along with Murray State All-American and future NBA star Joe Fulks, a 6-5 scoring machine. The San Diego Marine Corps Base team rattled off 35 consecutive wins, including a 55-42 victory over West Coast power Southern California.

"We had a bunch of great ball players. We had won 35 straight games and people said, 'Well, you didn't play anybody but service teams.' But we played the best service teams in the country," Sailors said. "I think we could have won the AAU Tournament pretty handily, because we had a collection of great ball players from all over the country."

The three Cowboys, dubbed the "Terrible Trio," even defeated Shelton's AAU team, Dow Chemical, which included Wyoming All-American center Milo Komenich.

"Shelton had to drop basketball at Wyoming for a year. He had Komenich there, and they came out to San Diego to play us. We beat them pretty handily. We didn't have trouble with them," Sailors said. "And everybody was predicting us to win the AAU tournament. Then we had a three-star general come home from the South Pacific and he had lost a son who was a second lieutenant and he was kind of bitter. You can't blame him. And here we were getting all this publicity and we're going to be the national champs. It didn't go over well with this old boy, not a bit. In the headline in the paper in San Diego he said, 'Are we playing basketball or are we fighting a war?' He says, 'I want these players out of here in 10 days.' And we headed out to the South Pacific."

Sailors' older brother Bud flew B-25s on missions near where Kenny was stationed in Guam. War was hell for everyone involved, and the star basketball player from Wyoming also had to deal with some guilt. Kenny admits that the military probably did what it could to avoid having the All-American and NCAA Tournament's Most Outstanding Player killed in combat.

"I lost a lot of my friends. In fact, I look back on it and it wasn't probably right. There's only one reason in the world I didn't have to go into Iwo Jima," Sailors said 66 years after nearly 7,000 Marines died during the key battle against the Japanese Imperial Army. "My outfit went in there and a lot of them didn't come back. But I think it had to do with my reputation as a ball player, I really do. I think that's why the Marines kept me out. You know, I had twice been the number 1 basketball player in the nation, which is picked by the coaches and sports writers. That wouldn't have been too good for the Marines when it comes to getting kids into the Marine Corps, if they got me shot up or killed. And there is a good chance it would have happened, a lot of my buddies died. So they kept me out of there, thank the Lord.

"In some ways, I feel kind of bad about it, too. I should have been over there with the other kids."

James W. "Jimmie" Reese was born on July 4, 1923, in Cumberland, Wyoming, a ghost town about 17 miles south of Kemmerer, Wyoming, which was once inhabited by employees and families of the Union Pacific Coal Company. After celebrating the national championship with the Cowboys, Reese served in the Naval Air Corps during World War II. Reese resumed his playing career at Wyoming following the war, leading the team in scoring (11.7 points per game) during the 1946-47 season and eventually playing on an AAU team. In 2003, Reese joined sailors and Lew Roney, who also joined the U.S. Navy and served in the Pacific during the war, at a Wyoming basketball game so the athletic department could honor the men for the 60th anniversary of their national championship. Roney, who was born on July 7, 1922, in Powell, Wyoming, died on Sept. 28. 2004. When Reese died on Oct. 14, 2010, the Associated Press obituary stated that "Kenny Sailors, of Laramie, is now the lone surviving member of Wyoming's 1943 NCAA championship team."

That was news to Tony Katana, a member of that famed Cowboys group who is alive and well in Green River. Katana, who grew up in Rock Springs, traveled with the Pokes throughout the 1942-43 campaign and even scored a career-high 20 points during Wyoming's 101-45 thrashing of Regis on Jan. 28, 1942.

"I went to Wyoming on a football scholarship to play for Bunny Oakes," Katana said. "I decided to try out for the basketball team for fun. I had no thought that I would actually make team."

Shelton saw enough in the 6-foot-3 walk-on to include Katana on the 10-man traveling team. He was the backup center to the 6-foot-7 Komenich. Katana saw action in 24 of Wyoming's 33 games that season.

"I thought we had special team, but I never dreamed or thought of winning the national championship," Katana said.

Katana received his draft card in the middle of the magical season and asked Shelton if he could leave the team to spend some time with his girlfriend (future wife) and family before his deployment in the 32nd Division of the U.S. Army Infantry.

"Shelton was a little bit pissed," Katana said. "But he understood the circumstances."

After Shelton, a World War I veteran, reluctantly granted the request, Katana missed Wyoming's trips to Kansas City and New York, where the Cowboys knocked off Oklahoma, Texas and Georgetown to win the NCAA title and then beat NIT champion St. John's for bragging rights as the country's undisputed number 1 team. But he was able to say goodbye to his loved ones back home before being shipped out to fight the Japanese on the coast of New Guinea.

"I don't regret it," Katana said of the decision. "I'd do the same thing again."

After returning home from the war in December of 1945, Katana married his high school sweetheart and went back to school at Wyoming, where he graduated with bachelor's and master's degrees in education. He spent three decades working as a teacher and principal in the Sweetwater (Wyoming) County School District. In 1983, Katana retired and was given a plaque and ring by the University honoring the 1943 national championship squad. If you stop by his house in Green River, the 89-year-old is quick to show off the hardware and happy to reminisce about his basketball playing days, or perhaps vent about the modern-day Cowboys' recent struggles on the hardwood.

"Playing on that team was a memory I will cherish to the end of my days," Katana said.

Sailors was honorably discharged with the rank of Captain and returned to Laramie in 1945. Some of the upperclassmen on Wyoming's 1943 NCAA championship squad had been awarded undergraduate degrees on their way to World War II, even if they were a little shy of all the necessary credits, just in case they never made it back home. So when Sailors rejoined the program during the 1945-46 season, he was considered a graduate student. Komenich averaged a team-high 14.3 points per game that season. Weir, who was wounded in combat and not quite the same player, also put on the Wyoming uniform again. The Cowboys picked up where they left off by winning their first 10 games of the campaign. That included another East Coast trip with a victory over Valparaiso in Buffalo, New York, and a win at St. Joseph's (Pennsylvania) in Philadelphia. On Jan. 3, 1946, Wyoming beat Long Island 57-42 at Madison Square Garden. The game was the subject of a spread in the Jan. 21, 1946, edition of *Life Magazine*, including a famous photograph of Sailors rising high above a defender to release the jump shot he had dazzled New York fans with three years earlier. The recap of the action read as follows:

> *As the basketball season approached the halfway mark last week, 14 of the 84 major U.S. college teams still remained undefeated. Head of the list was Wyoming University, which had won 10 consecutive games and seemed likely to emerge as the year's top team. Fortnight ago the*

Wyoming Cowboys made a long trek east and defeated Long Island University before a crowd of 18,056 people in New York's Madison Square Garden.

To win this game the Cowboys first had to neutralize the shooting skill of Jackie Goldsmith, Long Island ace forward and the season's high scorer in the New York area. This Wyoming accomplished by close guarding. Then, using the expert ball control of Milo Komenich and the fast, smooth dribble and the accurate jump shots of Kenny Sailors, the Cowboys went on to win 57-42.

The veteran Wyoming team uncharacteristically lost two home games in 1946 – the Skyline Conference opener to Utah on Jan. 12, and to BYU on Feb. 2. The Cowboys also lost back-to-back games at Oklahoma A&M, the eventual NCAA champions that season, on Jan. 25-26. But with a 10-2 record in conference play, Wyoming captured its third Skyline Conference title. However, despite winning 10 of their final 11 games, including a sweep of Colorado, and finishing with a 22-4 overall record, the Pokes were not invited to postseason play. The NCAA ruled that the program was ineligible to compete for a national title because Sailors and Weir were graduate students. The rival Buffs, who were 11-5 during the regular season and 9-3 in conference play, represented the Skyline Conference at the NCAA Tournament and lost to California in the first round.

"When Weir and I left we were short of graduation, and the university went ahead and graduated us. They probably thought they were doing our folks a favor in case we didn't come back," Sailors said. "They had a special ruling, the NCAA, that graduate students could play because most of us didn't play our freshman year. When it came tournament time, they said they wouldn't allow us to play. So they barred Wyoming. There were a lot of politics involved."

As a result of the ruling, the Cowboys, clearly one of the top teams in the nation, were denied the opportunity to win a second NCAA championship and the program's third national title. Sailors remained in the national spotlight, becoming the only three-time All-American in the program's rich history. In many ways, the 90-year-old legend is still the face of Wyoming basketball today. Sailors certainly deserves more national recognition for pioneering the jump shot and helping to popularize the NCAA Tournament.

"Wyoming is a storied program," former Wyoming head coach Jim Brandenburg said. "How many schools have won a national championship? Not that many, and Wyoming is one of them. How many schools have a coach in the Naismith Hall of Fame? Not too many, and Wyoming has one. And Kenny should also be in the Naismith or the National Collegiate Basketball Hall of Fame."

SOURCES

People Interviewed

Marcus Bailey, Keith Bloom, Turk Boyd, Jim Brandenburg, Tim Breaux, Irv Brown, Bud Daniel, Josh Davis, Benny Dees, Sean Dent, Stan Dodds, Brandon Ewing, Bob Hammond, Mike Jackson, Curt Jimerson, Tony Katana, Bob Kirchner, Eric Leckner, Steve McClain, Kevin McKinney, Theo Ratliff, Flynn Robinson, Kenny Sailors, Gregg Sawyer, Dick Sherman, Larry Shyatt, Reggie Slater, Jon Sommers and Tony Windis.

Sources

- Anderson, Richard. Hoops Reunion Brings Memories and Past Players Back to AA. Laramie Boomerang, Feb. 16, 2002.
- Associated Press. Member of 1943 UW basketball team dies, Oct. 14, 2010.
- Boulder Daily Camera, March 8, 1940.
- Branding Iron. Cowboy Reserves, Feb. 10, 1932.
- Burnley, Malcolm. Sailors And Steamrollers. The College Hill Independent, Oct. 29, 2010.
- Burns, Dr. Robert H. From the Samuel Howell Knight file at the American Heritage Center, University of Wyoming.
- Christgau, John. The Origins of the Jump Shot: Eight Men Who Shook the World of College Basketball. Lincoln: University of Nebraska Press, 1999.
- Copper River County Journal. From Madison Garden to Gakona Alaska! April 1, 1987.
- Crowe, Jerry. Flynn Robinson's life in basketball didn't end at 33. Los Angeles Times, March 24, 2008.
- Denver Nuggets. Kenny Sailors card, 1949-50 season.
- Eisenhauer, David. Old School: Cowboy basketball legend Kenny Sailors looks back on his rural upbringing, the 1943 championship season, and the shot that got the game off the ground. UWYO Magazine, Nov. 2005.
- Gagliardi, Robert. Back in the Game. Wyoming Tribune-Eagle, May 13, 2007.
- Hammond, Bob. Wyoming should properly recognize '34 team. Laramie Boomerang, Feb. 17, 2011; Cowboys in Chicago. Laramie Boomerang, May 12, 2011; Hall for the Hall. Laramie Boomerang, May 12, 2011; Katana 'alive and well' in Green River. Laramie Boomerang, Dec. 8, 2010; For Sawyer, Hall of Fame bid comes as a shock. Laramie Boomerang, June 25, 2010.

- Junge, Mark. Kenny Sailors Interview from the Final Four in Denver, March 30, 1990. Wyoming Department of State Parks & Cultural Resources archives. Transcribed and edited by Russ Sherwin, April 10, 2010.
- Kahn, Mike. Fennis Dembo is Wyoming's 'Electric Man.' The Sporting News, 1987-88 College Basketball Yearbook.
- Katz, Andy. A bittersweet triumph: Queint Higgins is playing again, but he wonders what might have been. The Sporting News, Feb. 14, 1994.
- KennySailorsJumpShot.com.
- Kirkpatrick, Curry. They're Jumping For Joy. Sports Illustrated, Nov. 18, 1987.
- Laramie Daily Bulletin. Tall Arkansans Whip Cowboys, 52-40. March 22, 1941; Welcome to the World's Champions of Basketball . . . The Wyoming Punchers. April 5, 1943.
- Latimer, Clay. Catching the Sport Flat-Footed. Rocky Mountain News, March 7, 2008.
- Lapchick, Richard E. 100 Pioneers: African-Americans Who Broke Color Barriers in Sport. Fitness Info Tech, 2008.
- Maloney, Tom. Aztecs fire Brandenburg. San Diego Union-Tribune, Feb. 12, 1992.
- Megargee, Steve. Fennis Dembo remains a name to remember. Rivals.com, July 23, 2006. Accessed at http://collegebasketball.rivals.com/content.asp?CID=563395.
- Meyer, Ray. Personal letter to Kenny Sailors. Undated.
- Moss, Irv. Colorado Classic: Coach Tom Asbury calls it a career. The Denver Post, March 15, 2011.
- Naismith Memorial Basketball Hall of Fame. Glenn Roberts and the Genesis of the Jump Shot. Accessed at http://hoophall.com/glenn-roberts-and-the-genesis/
- Nebraska High School Sports Hall of Fame. Les Witte, Lincoln. Accessed at http://www.nebhalloffame.org/2003/leswitte.htm.
- Nevius, C.W. Memory Lane not a Glory Road. San Francisco Chronicle, Jan. 24, 2006. Accessed at sfgate.com.
- O'Day, Joe. Mr. Basketball Prophesies A Bright New New York Era. New York Sunday News, March 14, 1965.
- O'Gara, Geoffrey. Wyoming's Gift to the Final Four. Wyoming Tribune-Eagle, April 3, 2010.
- O'Neil, Dana. Life not as easy as hoops for Dembo. ESPN.com, Sept. 29, 2009. Accessed at http://sports.espn.go.com/ncb/columns/story?columnist=oneil_dana&id=4512023.
- Pennington, Bill. In Search of the First Jump Shot. The New York Times, April 2, 2011.
- Porter, David L. Basketball: a biographical dictionary. Greenwood Press, 2005.

- Schmoldt, Eric. Still going strong: 89-year-old Sailors remains young at heart. Casper Star-Tribune, Jan. 24, 2010.
- Simers, T.J. and Brown, Brian. Aztecs to hire Brandenburg today. San Diego Union, March 24, 1987.
- Teitel, Jon. Q&A with Wyoming Great Fennis Dembo. Collegehoops.net. Accessed at: http://www.collegehoopsnet.com/qa-w-wyoming-great-fennis-dembo-168296
- Thorburn, Ryan. Black 14: The Rise, Fall, and Rebirth of Wyoming Football. Burning Daylight, 2009; In worst of times, these Buffs were one of best. The Boulder Camera, May 29, 2011.
- Time Magazine. Cowboys vs. Indians. April 12, 1943.
- Wetheim, L. Jon. SI Vault, Nov. 24, 1997. Accessed at http://sportsillustrated.cnn.com/vault/article/magazine/MAG10 11509/index.htm.
- Wojnarowski, Adrian. Winning at BYU is a black-and-white decision. ESPN.com, Feb. 24, 2003.
- University of Wyoming annual yearbooks, 1918-59. American Heritage and Emmett Chisum Library, special collections.
- Wyoming Basketball Media Guide. Compiled by the Wyoming Media Relations Office. Edited by Tim Harkins.
- Wyoming Athletics Hall of Fame. Accessed at http://www.wyomingathletics.com/genrel/wyo-hof.html
- Wyoming University Basketball Records. Compiled by Robert H. Burns. Emmett Chisum Library, special collections.
- Yantz, Tom. How The Jump Shot Got Its Start. The Hartford Courant, Nov. 26, 1993.
- Zeigler, Mark. Brandenburg now an Aztec. San Diego Union, March 25, 1987.
- Zieralski, Ed. Dees' Cowboys figure to sit tall in WAC saddle. The Sporting News, 1987-88 College Basketball Yearbook.

About Ryan Thorburn

Ryan Thorburn is a Sports Writer for the *Boulder Camera* with a degree in journalism from the University of Wyoming. He is the award winning author of *Black 14: The Rise, Fall, and Rebirth of Wyoming Football; Lost Cowboys: The Story of Bud Daniel and Wyoming Baseball;* and this his third book completing a sports trilogy—*Cowboy Up: Kenny Sailors, The Jump Shot and Wyoming's Championship Basketball History.* Mr. Thorburn currently lives in Westminster, Colorado with his wife Nicole, and three daughters, Madelyn, Gabrielle and Peyton.

Books by Pearn and Associates, Inc.

Novels:
1945, Joseph J. Kozma, (fiction), paper *
Another Chance, Joe Naiman, (fiction — publisher only) cloth
Light Across the Alley, *The Story of a Young Matchmaker,*
    Victor W. Pearn (fiction) Kindle Books only*
Point Guard, Victor Pearn (fiction) cloth

Nonfiction:
A Lenten Journey Toward Christian Maturity, William E.
    Breslin (prayer guide, also available in Spanish) paper
Black 14: The Rise, Fall and Rebirth of Wyoming Football,
    Ryan Thorburn (sports biography) paper
Cowboy Up: Kenny Sailors, The Jump Shot and Wyoming's Championship Basketball History,
    Ryan Thorburn, (sports biography) paper †
Dream Season, *My Brother Gary and the 1957 Ashland Panthers*
    Victor W. Pearn (sports biography) Kindle Books only*
Goulash and Picking Pickles, Louise Hoffmann (biography) cloth
Ikaria: A Love Odyssey on a Greek Island, Anita Sullivan
    (biography) paper *
I Look Around for my Life, John Knoepfle (biography) cloth*
It Started & Ended: The Story About a Soldier and Civilian Life,
    Bud Grounds (biography) paper
Lost Cowboys: The Bud Daniel Story, and Wyoming Baseball,
    Ryan Thorburn (sports biography) paper
The Great Adventure—UNTOLD, Charles Hamman, (nonfiction) cloth*

Poetry:
Mathematics in Color, Joseph J. Kozma (poetry) paper
The Dreamer and the Dream, Rick E. Roberts (poetry) paper
Until We Meet, Joseph J. Kozma (poetry) paper
Walking in Snow, John Knoepfle (poetry) paper

Available on Barnesandnoble.com, Amazon.com, (also available from Ingram Books, and Baker and Taylor) you may order at your local bookstore or directly from the publisher, Pearn and Associates, Inc. happypoet@hotmail.com. †Available on Nook; *Available on Kindle Books.

www.ingramcontent.com/pod-product-compliance
Lightning Source LLC
Chambersburg PA
CBHW070938180426
43192CB00039B/2319